Eastertide in Pennsylvania

Eastertide in Pennsylvania

A Folk-Cultural Study

Alfred L. Shoemaker

New Foreword and Afterword by
Don Yoder

STACKPOLE
BOOKS

Originally published in 1960 by the Pennsylvania Folklife Society
Foreword and Afterword © 2000 by Don Yoder

Published by
STACKPOLE BOOKS
5067 Ritter Road
Mechanicsburg, PA 17055
www.stackpolebooks.com

Printed in the United States of America

10 9 8 7 6 5 4 3 2 1

FIRST STACKPOLE EDITION

*Frontispiece: A photograph, taken by H. Winslow Fegley around the turn of the
century, of a Pennsylvania Dutch woman in the process of dyeing Easter eggs.*
SCHWENKFELDER LIBRARY

Library of Congress Cataloging-in-Publication Data

Shoemaker, Alfred Lewis, 1913–
    Eastertide in Pennsylvania : a folk-cultural study / Alfred L. Shoemaker ; new foreword
and afterword by Don Yoder. — 1st Stackpole ed.
        p.   cm.
    Includes bibliographical references and index.
    ISBN 0-8117-0548-X
    1. Easter—Pennsylvania.   2. Pennsylvania—Social life and customs.   I. Title.

GT4935.S5   2000
394.2667'09748—dc21   99–045374

Contents

Publisher's Note

In 1960 the Pennsylvania Folklife Society published Alfred L. Shoemaker's *Eastertide in Pennsylvania*, after releasing his *Christmas in Pennsylvania* the previous year. Four decades later Stackpole Books follows the same sequence: Having republished *Christmas in Pennsylvania* last year, we now present this new edition of *Eastertide in Pennsylvania*. Dr. Shoemaker's work remains a vibrant, accessible compilation of interviews and newspaper accounts on early folk practices associated with the spring holidays in the state, and Stackpole is proud to bring it back into print.

In this edition, the Shoemaker text has been reset with a new design. Minor corrections of spelling and punctuation have been made, but otherwise the content remains untouched.

Dr. Shoemaker's longtime colleague, Don Yoder, has contributed immensely to the project. He has offered a foreword, recounting the exhaustive accomplishments of that pivotal institution that he cofounded with Dr. Shoemaker, the Pennsylvania Folklife Society, and an afterword, providing a look at research on the springtime holidays and their European origins. In addition, Dr. Yoder has furnished translations of several Pennsylvania Dutch excerpts that had not been included in the original, supplied illustrations from his vast Roughwood Collection, compiled the extensive bibliography, and assisted me as a consultant on countless matters related to the book.

As *Eastertide in Pennsylvania* was first released as part of a grand mission to bring Pennsylvania's folk-cultural past to a popular audience, so too is this new edition part of a publishing plan: Stackpole's growing Pennsylvania line, committed to producing quality books, both new works and reprints of past treasures, such as this one, on Pennsylvania history, culture, and life.

KYLE R. WEAVER, EDITOR
JANUARY 2000

Foreword

In the 1950s Franklin and Marshall College in Lancaster, Pennsylvania, was the nerve center of Pennsylvania Dutch research. It was there in 1949 that Alfred L. Shoemaker, J. William Frey, and I, Don Yoder, three young professors who had converged on the college, founded a research institute that we called the Pennsylvania Dutch Folklore Center.

Modeling the center on folk-cultural institutes at German, Swiss, and Scandinavian universities, we launched an aggressive collecting program, combining fieldwork with historical ethnography, archiving materials of all sorts, and publishing significant results in the new periodical we founded in 1949, *The Pennsylvania Dutchman*.

To the periodical, we each contributed our specialties. Dr. Shoemaker offered materials on customs of the year, including papers done for his classes at the college, where he had founded the first Department of American Folklore in the United States. His wide-ranging interests included also folktales and jests, folk art, and bibliography, with listings of the German newspapers published in the nineteenth century for the Pennsylvania Dutch people. Dr. Frey headed the dialect department; we published his *Simple Grammar of Pennsylvania Dutch* serially, and later issued it in pamphlet form. He also contributed folksongs and other dialect materials. My area was Pennsylvania Dutch history and biography, religious history, and genealogy. My pages, called "Speaking of Families," attracted letters from all over the country from "Displaced Dutchmen" searching for their Pennsylvania roots.

The journal began ambitiously as a weekly, in folio format, and soon had a subscription list exceeding that of most folklore journals in the United States. I look back with pleasure on those long evenings spent editing the journal in our offices on the third floor of Fackenthal Library. Eventually, however, we rescheduled the journal as a monthly, not for lack of material, but for the good reason that all three of the editors had full-time teaching positions at the college.

We were soon joined in the library by another fascinating Dutchman, Dr. Harvey Bassler. Little, wizened, and weatherbeaten from his geologist years in search of oil in South America, he had made a fortune, part of which he spent buying the twenty-ton collection of Pennsylvaniana that had been amassed by Claude W. Unger of Pottsville. This massive trove of boxes and cabinets included books, pamphlets, newspapers, and folk art, among which was an unmatched store of Pennsylvania Dutch fraktur that Unger had bought at country sales when the price of each piece was a few dollars! All of this was deposited on the third floor of the library, and Dr. Bassler began to sort it, often staying there all night. Over time, the thousands of German imprints that Unger collected were catalogued by Wilbur H. Oda at the center's expense.

The genial Dr. Bassler was most supportive of our research program, and we were frequently able to use materials from the Unger-Bassler Collection, as it came to be called, in our publication. I cannot forget his oft-repeated phrase of encouragement, *"Waart juscht, waart juscht!"* ("Just wait, just wait!") as we talked over our extensive research plans for the future. We had planned to add to the Fackenthal Library a Bassler wing, which would also house the center's work, but alas, that was not to be. After Dr. Bassler's tragic death, along with that of another important scholar, Rudolf Hommel, in an automobile accident near West Chester in 1951, the collection was taken over by the college library, which kept the Pennsylvania Dutch materials but dispersed much unrelated material to other libraries.

Eventually, converted from the Anglo-American concept of folklore to the broader European concept of folklife, which embraces all aspects of traditional culture, we renamed the journal *Pennsylvania Folklife* in 1958, to do justice to all the ethnic, sectarian, and regional groups that make up Pennsylvania's population. With this change the journal became a quarterly, normally of forty-eight pages, highly and beautifully illustrated. *Pennsylvania Folklife* was the pioneer folklife journal in the United States and has served as a model for many state folklife periodicals. With this significant name change, we also incorporated our research center as the Pennsylvania Folklife Society.

In 1950 the center initiated the Pennsylvania Dutch Folk Festival at Kutztown, a locale chosen for its archetypical Pennsylvania Dutchness. In Berks County midway between Reading and Allentown, Kutztown was—and still is—the center of a charming rural area where many local residents were farmers and many of them knew and used Pennsylvania Dutch in their everyday communication. Under Dr. Shoemaker's creative direction, the festival attracted national attention; by 1960 it was drawing 100,000 visitors a year, making it the largest folk festival in the country. It was also the first folklife festival in the United States, and as such has influenced other festivals, including the National Festival of American Folklife in Washington, D.C.

The festival was in a very real sense an experiment in adult education. It offered visitors a chance to experience selected aspects of Pennsylvania Dutch farm life as demonstrated by local farmers and their wives, to talk with traditional craftsmen, to see Dutch folk dancing, and to hear folksongs sung in our dialect. Visitors could also sit down at friendly (and groaning!) tables to sample authentic Dutch farm cuisine served by congenial folk from nearby country churches and granges.

To educate the public in a more permanent way than was possible in a weeklong festival, we began a publication program. In addition to our journal, we published books and pamphlets on many subjects of Pennsylvania Dutch interest. In the first twelve years (1949–1961) we issued five hardback books, three by Alfred Shoemaker and two from my research.

First on the list was *Songs along the Mahantongo* (1951), on which I collaborated with Walter E. Boyer and Albert F. Buffington. Our materials were recorded in our ancestral Mahantongo culture area, north of Harrisburg, where Schuylkill, Dauphin, and Northumberland counties come together.

The next three books we published were *The Pennsylvania Barn* (1958) by Dr. Shoemaker, myself, and other contributors; *Christmas in Pennsylvania: A Folk-Cultural Study* (1959), reissued in 1999 by Stackpole Books in a fortieth-anniversary edition; and *Eastertide in Pennsylvania* (1960).

The last of our books was *Pennsylvania Spirituals* (1961), my collection of "bush meeting" songs of the revivalist Pennsylvania Dutch churches, which had been influenced by Anglo-American revivalism, as spread through Pennsylvania principally by Methodists. These included the denominations known as the United Brethren, the Evangelical Association and its progeny, the Churches of God, the Mennonite Brethren in Christ, and certain locally derived Holiness groups.

The list of pamphlets published by the center is even more impressive than its book list. Dr. Shoemaker contributed *Pennsylvania Dutch Hex Marks* (1952); *Three Myths about the Pennsylvania Dutch Country* (1951); and *Hex No!* (1953); also *Traditional Rhymes and Jingles* (1951); *Check List of Pennsylvania Dutch Printed Taufscheins* (1952); *My Off Is All* (1953), a joke book; *A Peek at the Amish* (1954); and *The Pennsylvania Dutch Country* (1954). Some of the titles were "cute," but the contents were solid, and many of these offerings are now collectors' items.

Dr. Frey contributed his *Pennsylvania Dutch Grammar* (1950) and *That Amazing Pennsylvania Dutch Language* (1951). In addition, there was a *Coloring and Design Book for Children of All Ages* (1951) by Olive G. Zehner and R. D. Dunkelberger. We also published several pamphlet cookbooks by Edna Eby Heller, *A Pinch of This and a Handful of That* (1951, with a second volume in 1952) and *Shoo-fly Cookery* (1953). For dialect buffs we offered several reprints of early Pennsylvania Dutch pamphlets from the 1860s and 1870s. Lastly, I joined Dr. Shoemaker in editing the 1954

and 1955 *Tourist Guide through the Dutch Country,* which became the model for several similar guides published elsewhere.

Educative, yes! It was the center's purpose to educate the public with attractive and readable yet scholarly publications on the true nature of the complex and fascinating Pennsylvania Dutch culture. This was not a "German island" in the New World but a vital American hybrid culture that combined elements brought from Continental Europe with contributions from the British Isles and America itself.

So we come to *Eastertide in Pennsylvania*. Based on the folklife approach using historical documentation plus fieldwork interviews, it presents the Pennsylvania Dutch spring festivals one after the other from Shrove Tuesday to Whitsuntide. It is our hope with this republication of Alfred Shoemaker's book that whole new generations of Americans can enjoy its delightful vignettes of the festival aspects of Pennsylvania Dutch folklife.

DON YODER
FASTNACHT 2000

Foreword to the First Edition

This study of Pennsylvania folklife from Shrove Tuesday through Whitmonday is a sequel to my *Christmas in Pennsylvania: A Folk-Cultural Study*, which appeared last year as the first annual publication of the Pennsylvania Folklife Society. Our purpose is to describe the traditional practices and folk beliefs attaching to Eastertide in the commonwealth.

Excluded from consideration are institutional practices as they pertain to these festivals of the Christian calendar, whether religious in nature (as in church or Sunday school) or secular (as in all their commercial aspects). Nor, we add, is this volume concerned with how the creative arts—music, literature, and painting—have utilized these days of the church year as a theme.

The reader should keep in mind that the majority of Pennsylvania's population was for a period of well-nigh two full centuries unfriendly to the celebration of these Christian festivals. In eighteenth-century Pennsylvania over two-thirds of the state's citizenry shunned their observance. Quakers and Scotch-Irish Presbyterians looked upon their being kept as church holidays in the Pennsylvania Dutch Country as "Dutch Popery," as one of them put it. Besides the Pennsylvania Dutch denominations, the only others which celebrated these days in the formative period of our history were the Episcopalians and the Catholics, but their numbers then were small and their influence, upon our overall folk culture, but slight.

It is quite obvious, therefore, that this study is actually the story of these festival days in the Pennsylvania Dutch Country.

ALFRED L. SHOEMAKER
1960

Introduction to the First Edition

The reader—if he wishes fully to comprehend the significance of the material here presented—needs to be quite clear as to what the word *culture* means as used by cultural anthropologists, ethnologists, folklorists, and other students of human society.

In simple terms, scholars in these disciplines define culture as one's social heritage. Generally speaking, cultural anthropologists concern themselves with the study of primitive society; ethnologists and folklorists, on the other hand, have as their concern our civilized societies.

The folklorist breaks culture down into two parts: one part comprising creative, individual social heritage; the other part consisting of traditional, group social heritage. Concretely, that which we learn formally in church or school—no matter what its level—is creative culture; that which we acquire informally—whether in the home, on the farm, or in the craftshop—we call folk culture.

Creative culture is primarily composed of the contributions of the *individual* to society—authors, painters, musicians. Folk culture, on the other hand, concerns group culture—the contributions of the farmer, the blacksmith, the builder of barns, all, you will note, nameless in the main.

Education, throughout history, has been limited overwhelmingly to studying what a Shakespeare has written, what a Rubens has painted. Only recently—within the past few scores of years—has scholarship turned to a study of the folktale (the author nameless and inconsequential) and to folk art (painters of our Pennsylvania Dutch chests, of our birth and baptismal certificates, of our barn signs, all unnamed artists for the most part).

Similarly, scholars are beginning—just now beginning—to break religion in our civilized societies down into two parts: one part religion as transmitted in church, Sunday school, or theological seminary; and folk religion, consisting of practices like powwowing and the whole realm of folk beliefs (which have disparagingly always been called "superstitions").

This volume, though we subtitle it a folk-cultural study, is in fact a major contribution to Pennsylvania Dutch folk religion.

The time is at hand no longer to sneer, but to collect and study, yes, to consider folk beliefs as dignified expressions of folk religion, worthy of academic study and deserving of general public tolerance and understanding.

We need to begin to fight for folk-religious tolerance, folk-religious tolerance of the type which found expression in the following utterance [written in 1910] of Dr. Ammon Stapleton, one of the greatest of our Pennsylvania church historians:

In using the word superstition in connection with religion, I have no doubt that it occurs to us how closely the terms have been identified in the ages past, and it is easy to see how closely the two ideas were allied. I know that within our own family, over near the foot of the Blue Mountains in old Dutch Berks some fifty-one years ago, we had customs that we would never think of now, but in those days they were a part of our life. On Green Thursday we would just as reverently and sacredly gather the eggs that were laid that day for Easter morning breakfast, and if there were not enough eggs to go around father would divide the portion so that each would have a taste of the eggs. This was a part of our religious belief. You may call it superstition if you please, but it was part of our religion and a custom that we followed regularly every year until I was a grown-up man.

Then father would take us out in the fields and we would go through the fields hunting for different herbs which were a cure for certain diseases. And in that practical way I learned what has never been taken from me. After I was a high school boy I learned the technical part of botany, but the foundation was laid when I was a child. Snake root, sarsaparilla—all these things we gathered and they were just as much a part of our religion as we said our prayers, and we kept them to be used during the year for fever or any disease that we might be threatened with.

ALFRED L. SHOEMAKER
1960

SHROVE TUESDAY

Shrove Tuesday and Christmas have one thing in common in the Pennsylvania Dutch Country: They are two days in the year when the kiddies get up unusually early. On Christmas it is to see what Kriss Kringle has brought; on Shrove Tuesday morning the children get up early because the last one out of bed is called the *fastnacht* (pronounced "faws(a)nacht" in dialect) and is teased unmercifully all day long, not only by the members of his family but by his schoolmates as well.

Besides the word *fastnacht* for the last riser on Shrove Tuesday morning, there are also other terms[1] that one comes upon in the dialect, though these are more regional in character. There is also a word in some areas of Dutch-speaking Pennsylvania for the one who gets up first on the morning of this day.

In Northampton, Monroe, and Carbon counties I have collected the word *der haus-lumba* (the cleaning rag) as a name for the member of the family who is the first out of bed on Shrove Tuesday morning. In Schuylkill and Dauphin counties the first one up is called *die gluck* (the cluck). A Mrs. William E. Werner, an elderly woman, of Jefferson, York County, told the author in 1953 that the last one up was *die faws* and the first one *die alt asch*. Mrs. Harry Senft of the same place says in their family the first one up was called *der gansert* (the gander). And Mrs. Willis Burns, also of Jefferson, relates how her mother came to her rescue when her brother teased her overmuch as the fastnacht. Her mother told her to call him, the first riser on Shrove Tuesday morning, *der schpeel-lumba-suckler* (the dishrag sucker).

In 1952 I spoke at the annual Fastnacht Party held in the social rooms of the First Church of the Brethren in York. After my talk a Mrs. Anna Trimmer, formerly of the Dover area of the county, came up to report that as a child she used to hear the word *faws-gluck* (fastnacht cluck) for the last one up on Shrove Tuesday morning. In 1949 when I was writing a triweekly folklore column in the Lancaster *New Era* I had a letter from a Dr. Colsin R. Shelly of Lancaster, a native of western York County, who wrote me:

The last one out of bed on Shrove Tuesday was the old cluck, the first one the little *peepie*. The last one at school was the old cluck and was frequently reminded of the fact during the day by calling him the old cluck.

Additional light is thrown on this whole fastnacht cluck matter in a letter I had a number of years ago from an aged lady, Sarah B. Adam, of the Fleetwood section of Berks County. She wrote:

On *Fawsenacht* morning the schoolhouse shutters were closed. It appeared from a distance as though no one were inside. But when one came almost to the door he heard differently, for from the inside came a strange noise. The girls were cackling like hens and the boys were crowing like roosters. "Hello *fawsenacht*," one or the other finally called out and after a little ribbing, you were let in.

Instructions were then imparted to the last comer. They were: when the next pupil comes you may not cackle or crow as we do or else you will have to pay a forfeit; you are the one who has to call out "hello *fawsenacht*" a dozen or so times.

When the next pupil arrived, the same ceremony was repeated. Close tab was kept of those who broke the rules, for those pupils had to pay a forfeit.

1

Finally the teacher arrived. There was a general cackling and crowing called "*Du bischt die fawsenacht.*" The shutters were opened. Then came the time when the forfeits had to be paid. This is when the fun really began. Some of the boys had to stand on their heads, others had to walk on their hands.

The girls who had to pay forfeits were told to go and sit on the teacher's lap and give him a kiss. One of the older girls, I remember, wasn't slow. She went and sat on teacher's lap, reached around his neck, hugged him good and kissed him. The teacher got as red as a beet.

Did we children laugh! I never heard more laughter than on *Fawsenacht* morning at school.

The fastnacht cluck of Pennsylvania may hark back to English grammar school customs such as the sport of throwing at cocks and hens on Shrove Tuesday.

The most welcome thing about Shrove Tuesday is the special kind of doughnut, which is tradition-ally baked on this day in the Pennsylvania Dutch Country. This specialty goes by the name fast-nachts. Among families that hold to the old ways fastnachts are rectangular in shape with a slit in the middle. In recent decades, as commercial bakeries have taken over the making of fastnachts, they have taken on the round doughnut shape. In fact, many of the church groups that annually bake fast-nachts to raise money are now also serving them doughnut-shape, perhaps for uniformity's sake.

Just as there is no one shape for fastnachts, so is there no agreement as to whether a fastnacht is properly made with raised or unraised dough. It all seems to depend on the area where one was raised. In my native Lehigh County I grew up where only unraised fastnachts were made and always in the traditional rectangular shape. When I came to live in Berks and Lancaster counties, the raised kind was customary. Women in York County tell me a fastnacht is always made of raised dough, that doughnuts of unraised dough are properly called

grenslin in York County Dutch. A check of the local cookbooks in the York County Historical Society shows that in each instance the recipe for fastnachts calls for raised dough.

Of course, fastnachts, like all other cakes in the Dutch Country, must be dunked to be really good. In Lancaster and Lebanon counties—our saffron belt—they are dunked in saffron tea. Mrs. J. R. Cresswell, of Morgantown, West Virginia, wrote us at the Folklife Society some years ago:

The most delightful use we put saffron to was on Shrove Tues-day when we put it in tea. For supper on that day we always had fastnachts—big, rectangular ones, with lots of air holes inside them. You split the fastnacht, filled the holes up with molasses and then dunked them in the saffron tea. The only time I get really homesick to be back on the farm is on Shrove Tuesday evening.

Saffron tea may be all right for someone who has his roots in the western section of our Dutch-land. As for me, there is nothing that can compare with good old blue balsam tea. Naturally, the fast-nachts must be dripping molasses before they are really dunkable.

Back in 1948 I ran a triweekly column, "Old Berks Folklore, Legends and History," in the Read-ing *Eagle*. At the time I wrote a fictitious letter (signed Fastnacht Purity League) in which I expressed rather vehement opposition to church groups serving *round* fastnachts. This prompted Raymond E. Hollenbach, a native of Saegersville, Lehigh County, to reply as follows:

The shape of the *fastnacht kuche* has nothing at all to do in determining whether the product is genuine or not. The deter-mining factor is whether or not it is baked with yeast. If it is baked with yeast, it is just an ordinary doughnut, regardless of whether it is round, square, triangular, or whatever the shape may be. The hole in the center is also immaterial. That is merely put there to insure thoroughness in baking.

Fastnachts (pronounced "faws-nachts" in dialect) are served each Shrove Tuesday throughout Pennsylvania Dutch Country. Traditionally they are baked in a rectangular shape, with a slit through the middle.

A genuine *fastnacht kuche* is made WITHOUT yeast. This is important. Shrove Tuesday is a religious holiday and the absence of yeast was considered very important by our ancestors. Another thing, *fastnacht kuche* are baked only once a year—on Shrove Tuesday or on the Monday before. The important thing is that they be eaten on Shrove Tuesday, although a sufficient quantity is generally baked to last the rest of the week, provided the family appetite is not too large. Anything baked with raised dough is NOT a *fastnacht kuche* regardless of when it is baked or how it is shaped.

For future reference, I am giving you herewith a recipe for genuine *fastnacht kuche:*

3/4 cup of thick sour cream
3/4 cup of thick sour milk
1/4 cup of sugar
1 egg
1 1/2 teaspoonful baking soda

Stiffen with enough flour to roll. Roll about 1/4 inch thick and cut into desired shape and size—two-inch squares are preferable. Fry in deep fat. The amount of sugar may be made larger, but this is not necessary if eaten in the approved manner.

To eat, split the *fastnacht kuche* in half and fill the inside with *gwidde hunnich* (quince jam). To use anything as ordinary and common as molasses on a genuine *fastnacht kuche* is an abomination. In the absence of *gwidde hunnich,* crab apple jelly may be substituted, but in our house we always have the foresight to have on hand at least one jar of *gwidde hunnich* just for this occasion.

This recipe has been used in our family, to my own knowledge, for four generations, and tradition says it was brought from Europe. Surely there must be Berks County homes where it is still used. My mother's family (Metzger) originated in Maxatawny, and old Mrs. Miller (wife of Dr. A. S. Miller), in whose kitchen I was privileged to eat *fastnacht kuche* many years ago, came from Albany in Berks County. My wife's family, which originated in Maidencreek and Richmond townships, were not acquainted with the recipe, but I have introduced it and anyone coming to our house on Shrove Tuesday will find the genuine product.

So much on the subject: raised versus unraised fastnachts. The "dispute" will have served a most worthwhile purpose, I feel, if it has succeeded in highlighting the vast folk-cultural variations that exist in the Dutch Country, from region to region, from community to community, yes, even from family to family. Nowhere, of course, are these differences so marked as they are in the culinary patterns.

In some farm families the first fastnachts that were baked were always fed to the chickens. Mrs. John Beaver, of Kratzerville, Snyder County, tells me the old-timers used to lay a plow line in a circle and then they crumbled the first three fastnachts in it for the chicken. The folk belief was that if one did this the hawks would not fetch the chickens or chicks in spring. Mrs. Amelia Hildenbrand, of the Mount Carmel area, says her mother cut up the first three fastnachts for the chickens because she believed this would make them lay more eggs. This same theme is contained in a dialect poem, *"Der Fahsnocht"* by J. J. Behney,

which appeared in the Lebanon *Evening Report* of February 28, 1900:

> *Der airsht kucha bockdt die mudder brow,*
> *Un feedert 'n im oldta verdrow;*
> *Es mocht die hinkle heftich layga,*
> *Die hawna halleluyer graya.*

> [Mother bakes the first cake brown,
> And feeds it in the ancient trust
> That it makes the chickens lay lots of eggs,
> And the rooster will crow "Hallelujah!"]

Mr. Victor C. Dieffenbach, of Bethel, Berks County, in an article "Fairies and Fastnachts" (*Pennsylvania Dutchman*, February 15, 1953, page 3), wrote:

On Shrove Tuesday my Grandmother used to say, "If you put the three first fastnachts you bake out on the window sill, where neither dogs nor cats can get at them, a fairy will come. You must put them there before daybreak and say nothing to anyone. If they disappear it means the fairy ate them and you will have good luck all year long.

The fat in which the fastnacht cakes were fried was believed to have more than ordinary power. W. J. Buck, in an article "Manners and Customs" in the 1884 *History of Montgomery County* (page 337), wrote:

The lard in which the cakes [were] fried would be preserved as possessing extraordinary virtues in healing sores. Wagons also were greased with it for hauling home the harvest, it being considered efficacious in checking the ravages of rats, mice, and insects.

On a folklore-collecting trip to Snyder County in 1951, a Mrs. John Minium told me her grandmother, Mrs. Jake Steffen, of Mt. Pleasant Mills, used to say if you greased the wheels of a wagon with the fat in which the fastnachts were fried, you wouldn't be bothered with rats. A Mrs. George Schroeder, of Albany Eck, Berks County, told me

The last one out of bed Shrove Tuesday morning is the fastnacht in Pennsylvania Dutch homes. It is clear who is the fastnacht in the illustration—father. An illustration by Eleanor Barba from "'S Pennsylfawnisch Deitsch Eck," a column edited by Dr. Preston A. Barba for many years in the Allentown Morning Call.

in 1955 that the fastnacht lard was rubbed on a cow's udder if it was sore. Henry Bailey of the same locality says this lard was used if a horse had a sore. He said also if a lumberman cut himself with an axe, there was nothing better for the wound than fastnacht fat. Mr. Bailey told me in his section the farmers greased the spindles of their farm wagons in the belief that this would prevent any of the horses from becoming fractious. I have frequently been told that folks always greased their garden spades with fastnacht lard before starting to dig their gardens in the belief that this practice would protect the vegetables from harmful insects and bugs. A Mrs. Viola Hahn, of Palmerton, Carbon County, told me a number of years ago that her mother always followed this practice and that one

year she neglected for some reason or other to follow the custom and that they were sorely troubled that summer with insects and worms getting at their *gawrda-sach* (vegetables).

Our Pennsylvania Dutch folklore has it that ill luck will befall a family in which fastnachts are not served on Shrove Tuesday. An elderly woman in Richland, Lebanon County, once told me that anyone who did not eat fastnachts on Shrove Tuesday wold suffer from boils. Miss Esther Moser, of Bally, Berks County, reports a folk belief in her section to the effect that eggs will not hatch under a chicken in a family which neglects to serve fastnachts on this day. W. J. Buck in an article "Manners and Customs" in the 1884 *History of Montgomery County* (page 337) wrote:

To neglect the making of those cakes on this day [fastnacht] would cause failure in the flax crop. In some cases, to help secure good long flax, an abundance would be baked and freely dealt out among friends and neighbors.

Just as the failure to eat fastnachts was believed to portend ill luck, so the partaking of them was supposed assure fine crops, especially a fine flax crop. Phebe Earle Gibbons, in her volume *Pennsylvania Dutch* (1874 edition, page 55), wrote:

A neighbor has told me that the people here used to make fat-cakes—they called them "plow-lines"—on Shrove Tuesday, or else "they conceited the flax wouldn't grow."

George F. Moore, of Lebanon County, reports a folk belief in his section that if you want to grow large heads of cabbage you must be sure to eat a lot of fastnachts on Shrove Tuesday.

Fastnacht frolics were a popular institution in the Dutch Country in the first half of the last century. Walter J. Hoffman, in an article on Pennsylvania Dutch folklore in the 1889 *Journal of American Folklore* (page 24), wrote:

Dances were held on Shrove-Tuesday "for a good yield of flax for that year," or, in other words, the host's crop of flax would be tall in proportion to the height to which the dancers raised their feet from the floor.

In my index of advertisements in the Kutztown *Geist der Zeit* I find a reference to a fastnacht frolic held on February 8, 1841, at the house of David Grath, in Kutztown. Robert K. Buehrle in an article "The Swamp of Tinicum and Nockamixon" (*Proceedings of the Bucks County Historical Society,* 1917, volume 4, page 88) wrote: "The usual time for dances was New Year's day and Shrove Tuesday, known as Fassnacht."

The late George Hartman, of Hamburg, Berks County, once told me his grandmother used to tell him of a fastnacht frolic at which the following folksong was sung:

Es ischt net all-tseit luschdich laiva,
Es ischt nicht all-tseit fawsanacht.
Ich hab mei geld em schpeelmann gaiva
Un hab gedrawmt die gansa nacht.

[Life isn't a merry round all the time.
Not every day of the year is Shrove Tuesday.
I gave my money to the fiddler
And I dreamed all night long.]

A complete version of this folksong, along with the music, collected in Central Pennsylvania, appears on pages 75–76 of the anthology of Pennsylvania Dutch folksongs *Songs along the Mahantongo* by Walter E. Boyer, Albert F. Buffington, and Don Yoder, published by the Pennsylvania Dutch Folklore Center in Lancaster in 1951.

Within recent years fastnacht socials have come into popularity in certain sections of the Dutch Country. The movement seems to have arisen in York County. A number of years ago the York County Historical Society began holding a social meeting on Shrove Tuesday, which they too call their Fastnacht Social.

Besides the fastnacht folksong of which there has already been mention, our popular oral literature uses the fastnacht theme but rarely. One of the best known riddles is *Well iss die lengscht nacht im yawr?* (What is the longest night in the year?) The answer is *Die fawsnacht, funwaiya siss aw fawsnacht im dawg.* (Fastnacht, because it is also *nacht*—night, that is—during the daytime.)

Of someone who is poorly informed on a subject, we apply the proverb *Er wais so wennich defun ass wie die pan fun fawsnacht.* (He knows as little about it as a pan knows about fastnacht.)

As on the other religious holidays in the Dutch Country, there is a work taboo on Shrove Tuesday. William Reinert, of near Fredericksville, Berks County, tells me if you sew on fastnacht you will sew up the hens' cloacae and prevent them from laying eggs. Victor C. Dieffenbach, of Bethel, recalls the old-timers saying that if a woman sewed on Shrove Tuesday, the snakes would invade her house in spring and summer. A Schuylkill countian once told me the old-time lumbermen did not like to work on Shrove Tuesday because they had a belief that if they cut themselves with an axe on this day, the wound would never heal. In Berks County there is the belief that one should not use an instrument with a sharp edge on Shrove Tuesday, for the same reason as above: Any wound from it would not heal.

Mrs. Viola Hahn, of Palmerton, told me that her mother, the late Mrs. David Rehrig, of Carbon County, believed one should get up early on Shrove Tuesday morning, not say a word to anyone, and go out in the yard stark naked. By doing this she believed she would not contract a disease during the course of the year. Mrs. Hahn tells good-humoredly that she one time told her milk man about this just before Shrove Tuesday and that on fastnacht morning at four-thirty she found his truck parked in the alley behind their house to see the "sights."

In the Lehigh Valley and sporadically elsewhere in the Dutch Country, Shrove Tuesday was the traditional day for barring out the schoolmaster. Elsewhere in the commonwealth the pupils locked out their teacher on or just before Christmas. The motive was twofold: to demand a Christmas gift and to force the schoolmaster to declare a school holiday. (For a detailed account of barring out the schoolmaster on Christmas, see my book *Christmas in Pennsylvania*.)

Phebe Earle Gibbons, in her book *Pennsylvania Dutch* (1882 edition, page 420), wrote:

An acquaintance, born in Northampton County, tells me that at his native place the teacher was locked out not at Christmas, but on Shrove-Tuesday, and merely for sport.

This custom was kept up until the mid-thirties of this century. It survived longest in the northern townships of Northampton County.

Barring out the schoolmaster was a custom introduced it seems from the British Isles. *Chamber's Book of Days* (volume 1, page 238) gives us a detailed account of a barring-out on Shrove Tuesday at Bromfield in Cumberland, England.

ASH WEDNESDAY

As on Shrove Tuesday, the last one out of bed in a family on Ash Wednesday morning was given a nickname. He or she became the *escha-puddel*. The word *esch* is dialect for ashes. In those areas of Southeastern and Central Pennsylvania where the dialect disappeared before the custom, the last riser was dubbed "the ash-pile."

The *escha-puddel* was always in for a highly unpleasant day. In addition to being teased by one's family all day long, one also got his face rubbed with ashes, not once or twice, but often and by all members of the family.

To be the family *escha-puddel* was bad enough in itself. If on this morning one happened to be so unfortunate as to be the last one to arrive at school before the last bell, he was really in for something. The whole school made fun of the unhappy victim and, what was worse, that pupil, if a boy, was rolled in the school ash pile by the other boys.

On Shrove Tuesday and Ash Wednesday in the Pennsylvania Dutch Country the boys and girls started on their way to school very early in the morning, some even before daybreak. Nobody, quite obviously, wanted to be the school *escha-puddel*. In some sections the school *escha-puddel* automatically fell heir to the undesirable job of carrying out the ashes, not just for that day but during the entire term.

In many of the Pennsylvania Dutch customs and folk beliefs one detects Catholic origin. The Reformation tried to do away with all Catholic folk practices, but what actually happened is that they were forced underground and many of them survive to this day in what I like to call "the ecclesiastical underworld," otherwise known as superstitions.

A Pennsylvania Dutch practice, clearly harking back to pre-Reformation days is that of ashing the cattle. Clayton N. Fidler, a Laureldale, Berks County, informant, described the custom in these words:

On *escha-puddel* day the master of the house got up early in the morning and never spoke a word to anyone until he got a bucket of ashes and went all over his livestock, missing none, and sprinkled everything with ashes. This was supposed to keep his livestock free from lice for the year.

That careful observer of Pennsylvania Dutch folklife, Phebe Earle Gibbons, makes note of the custom of ashing the cattle on Ash Wednesday in her remarkable volume, *Pennsylvania Dutch* (1874 edition, page 56):

Seven years ago I witnessed a sale of a large stock of cattle, on Ash Wednesday; every cow and steer offered for sale was completely covered with wood ashes.

Not only was the livestock ashed, including the "feather" stock, but also the garden, even the fruit trees. An elderly woman in DeTurksville in Schuylkill County a number of years ago told me she always scattered ashes over her garden on Ash Wednesday to keep away the insects. She said one year she neglected for some reason or other to ash and her garden was full of green thrips that year. Ever thereafter, she assured me, she never failed to ash her garden on Ash Wednesday.

In 1954 Els Hetrick, of Grantville, Dauphin County, a ninety-four-year-old man, told me they used to sprinkle ashes in the garden on Ash

Wednesday, first from north to south and then from east to west, so that a cross was made.

When one questions our farm folk as to the reason why the livestock is ashed—and the custom has now all but disappeared—he invariably gets the answer: "Why to *choke* the lice to death." This, I should say, proves that our Pennsylvania Dutch farmers have now really turned solid rationalists.

In Jefferson, York County, I collected the folk belief that if one strewed ashes all the way around the house on Ash Wednesday, no snake would enter the house for the ensuing year. An eighty-year-old woman put it this way: "If one makes a ring of ashes around the house on Ash Wednesday no snake can come inside of that ring."

One of our dialect poets, J. J. Behney, put our Ash Wednesday lore into a poem. It appeared in the Lebanon *Evening Report* of February 28, 1900. I reproduce it here in its original orthography.

Der dawg noch "Shrift-tseit" ward ganond,
Der esha-Midwuch we sis uns bakondt.

Es is der onfong's dawg der fosht,
Tsu moncha leit an groser losht.

Es wore d' gabrouch in oldta tseit
Tsu esha by da Ramer leit.

Der Bawbsht der shtawbdt die in der boose,
Un reinichdt olly kup un foose.

Dale hava aw tsum oldta glawva
In uns'ra tseit es fee tsu shtawva.

Der esha-puddle eshdt es fee,
Verdilgdt domit die lice uf kee.

Ferleichdt dute es am fee ken shawt
Es esha bodt won mer draw glawbt.

[The day was still called "Shrovetide,"
Ash Wednesday as it's known to us.

It's the opening day of the Lenten fast,
To many folks a heavy burden.

It was the custom in ancient times,
For the Roman people to scatter ashes.

The Pope used to dust those doing penance,
Thus purifying every head and foot.

Many still cling to the old belief,
And even in our times dust their cattle.

The *Eschepuddel** ashes the cattle,
And with it exterminates lice on the cows.

Perhaps it does the cattle no harm,
The ashing helps when you believe in it.]

Here and there one also comes upon a name for the last riser on the remaining three days of the first week in Lent. On Thursday one is *der schpeel-lumba-suckler* (the dishrag sucker). This term is rather widely known, it seems, but is restricted to the western area of the Dutch Country—the counties that lie west of the Schuylkill. In Berks County I collected the name *kee-schwantz* (cow's tail) for the last person to get up on Thursday; in Franklin County it's "the pig tail." William McQuate, of Reamstown, tells me that in his family the last one up on Thursday of the first week in Lent was called *der sei-kivvel-reider* (the swill-bucket rider). Solomon L. Grill of the same place told me in his family the last riser on Thursday was called *der sei-gnoddel* (the pig turd). Mrs. Maggie Adams, of Lebanon, who was reared near Indiantown Gap, says in her family they always called the last one up on Thursday following Ash Wednesday *die bree-gluck* (the brooding hen).

In certain areas of the Dutch Country the custom of giving a nickname was continued even Friday and Saturday of the first week in Lent. I have found these names in Lancaster and Lebanon counties only: *der sei-kivvel-reider, der bett-schtolla-reider* (the bedpost rider), *der panna-schlecker* (the pan licker), *der rung-gunkel*. Just what a *rung-gunkel* is I have not been able to find out.

The reader will no doubt have asked himself by this time—Where do all these names come from? To seek the answer one will have to go back several hundred years—to Germany and Switzerland, from where many of our customs come. There, on Shrove Tuesday, to this day people disguise themselves, much as we do on Halloween and as they do at the Mardi Gras in New Orleans. At one time, students of European folklife tell us, the costume with a cow's tail was very common. It is possible that our *kee-schwantz* (cow's tail), the name for the child who got out of bed last on Thursday in the first week in Lent, is a vague folk memory of a centuries-old parade.

It is not the purpose of this volume to seek out the European roots of our customs; this is a task that should be undertaken at some time, however. Only after this has been carefully done will we be able to determine what is indigenous in our lore and what was brought along by the immigrant generations.

MAUNDY THURSDAY

The dialect name for Maundy Thursday, *Grie(ner)-Dunnerschdawg* (Green Thursday, literally), is in very large part responsible for the basic lore that attaches to this day: One must eat something green on this day.

Dandelion was the green most commonly eaten. It assured one good health for the year, it was believed. Failure to eat something green on Maundy Thursday had dire consequences, according to the folk mind: One would get the itch, one would become lousy, or as a York County informant put it, *"Mer iss s gans yawr uff em aisel."* (One will be a mule all year long.)

Professor H. O. Werner, of the University of Nebraska, a Pennsylvania native, summed up the "Green Thursday" lore in an article in the *Pennsylvania Dutchman* of August 1, 1951, as follows:

I recall a superstitious custom which was in vogue up in the neighborhood of Wernersville, which was somewhat as follows: Each year the people would get out on that day in great numbers searching the grassy areas for dandelion plants. The accompanying belief with many of them was that anyone who would eat something green on Green Thursday would not be "sick of a fever" during the coming spring and summer. As so often happens, some of these superstitions would have some basis of fact. In this case, of course, over the years the people that indulged in the use of dandelion greens early in the spring and summer quite probably made up for a nutritional deficit which had developed during the long winters of limited diets. We know now that the dandelion leaves contain a very large amount of iron and a number of the essential vitamins, all of which were lacking in the winter meals, especially the latter part of winter.

In some instances in our Pennsylvania Dutch lore the number of greens one ate took on importance. Seven and nine were the magic numbers. By way of illustration, Don F. Geschwindt, a former student of mine, collected the following item (*Pennsylvania Dutchman*, April 1, 1951):

Mrs. Sallie Adams, of Shoemakersville, said that it was the tradition at their home to eat nine different kinds of "greens." These greens usually included dandelion, endive, turnip tops, cabbage, alfalfa, clover, etc.

Not only was one to eat something green on Maundy Thursday, one was also to wear something green, at least according to informants Mrs. Elda Herman, of Slate Valley, and Mrs. Ira Marsh, of near Danielsville, both communities located in Northampton County.

In our Pennsylvania Dutch folklore, next in importance to eating something green on Maundy Thursday is eating an egg for Easter Sunday breakfast that was laid on Maundy Thursday. William Master, of Mt. Pleasant Mills, Snyder County, told me on February 28, 1953:

At home we always ate the eggs laid on Maundy Thursday on Easter for breakfast. One should eat an egg laid on Maundy Thursday on Easter morning before breakfast to keep the fever away. I follow this custom to this day.

I encountered a similar bit of lore in the *Proceedings of the Pennsylvania German Society* (1910, volume 21, page 32). The late Edwin M. Fogel, then professor at the University of Pennsylvania, read a paper entitled "Some Pennsylvania-German Superstitions" at the twentieth meeting of the

Der Vierte Monat, Aprilis,

Woche Tage.	Merkwürdige Tage.	H. W.	Monds-Aufg.	Monds-Zeichen	Mondsch. Aspecten der Planet. und Witterung.	Uhr Taf.	Sonnen Auf- und Unterg.		Alter März.
						Uhr früh.	u. m.	u. m.	
freyt	1 Theodora	12	4 48	♓ 20	7* g. unt. 10, 10.				21 Benedictus
samst	2 Theodosia	1	5 29	♈ 3	‡ ☁ veränderlich,	3	5 42	6 18	22 Paulina
14] Lätare. JEsus speiset 5000 Mann. Joh. 6. Tagslänge 12 st. 36 minuten.									
Son	3 Ferdinand	2	d. ☽	♈ 15	d. 3t. sicht. ⊙	2	5 40	6 20	23 Eberhard
mont	4 Ambrosius	3	g. unt.	♈ 27	Finsterniß.	2	5 39	6 21	24 Gabriel
dienst	5 Maximus	3	8 30	♉ 9	temperirtes und	2	5 38	6 22	25 Mar. Ver.
mitw	6 Egesippus	4	9 28	♉ 21	☌ ♀ ☿ unschlach-	1	5 37	6 23	26 Emanuel
donn	7 Aaron	5	10 25	♊ 3	☌ ♄ ♂ tiges	1	5 35	6 25	27 Gustavus
freyt	8 Dionysius	6	11 21	♊ 15	☌ ♄ ☿ April-	1	5 34	6 26	28 Gideon
samst	9 Prochorus	7	Morg.	♊ 27	wetter mit	0	5 33	6 27	29 Eustatius
15] Judica. Die Juden wollen JEsum steinigen. Joh. 8. Tagsl. 12 st. 54 m.									
Son	10 Daniel	7	1 9	♋ 8	schlossen,	0	5 32	6 28	30 Guido
mont	11 Julius	8	2 0	♋ 20	☾ den 11ten	0	5 30	6 30	31 Detlaus
dienst	12 Eustachius	9	2 47	♌ 3	unbeständig	0	5 29	6 31	1 April
mitw	13 Justinus	10	3 29	♌ 16	☌ ⊙ ☿ und wie	Uhr später.	5 28	6 32	2 Theodosia
donn	14 Tyburtius	11	4 2	♌ 29	es um diese	0	5 26	6 34	3 Ferdinand
freyt	15 Olympia	11	4 44	♍ 13	♀ g. unt. 8, 38.	0	5 25	6 35	4 Ambrosius
samst	16 Calixtus	12	5 7	♍ 28	✱ ♃ ♀ zeit zu	0	5 24	6 36	5 Maximus
16] Palmsont. Vom Einritt Christi. Matth. 21. Tagsl. 13 st. 12 m.									
Son	17 Rudolph	1	5 34	♎ 12	seyn pflegt,	1	5 23	6 37	6 Egesippus
mont	18 Aeneas	2	der ☽	♎ 27	d. 18t. unf. ⊙	1	5 22	6 38	7 Aaron
dienst	19 Anicetus	2	g. auf	♏ 12	✝ ☁ finst.	1	5 20	6 40	8 Dionysius
mitw	20 Sulpitius	3	8 40	♏ 27	⊙ in ♉ heftige	1	5 19	6 41	9 Prochorus
donn	21 Gründonn.	4	9 37	♐ 12	✝ ☁ winde doch	1	5 18	6 42	10 Daniel
freyt	22 Charfreyt.	5	10 31	♐ 27	✝ ☁ gewächsig,	2	5 17	6 43	11 Julius
samst	23 Georgius	6	11 22	♑ 11	☽ leidlich und	2	5 16	6 44	12 Eustachius
17] Ostern. Von der Auferstehung Christi. Marc. 16. Tagsl. 13 st. 28 m.									
Son	24 Ostersont.	6	Morg.	♑ 26	lieblich wetter,	2	5 15	6 45	13 Justinus
mont	25 Ostermont.	7	1 3	♒ 9	☽ den 25sten.	2	5 13	6 47	14 Tyburtius
dienst	26 Cletus	8	1 52	♒ 23	‡ ☁ warme	2	5 12	6 48	15 Olympia
mitw	27 Anastasius	9	2 19	♓ 5	7* g. unt. 8, 40.	2	5 11	6 49	16 Calixtus
donn	28 Vitalis	10	2 43	♓ 17	✝ ☁ regen und	3	5 9	6 51	17 Rudolph
freyt	29 Sybilla	11	3 8	♈ 0	✱ ♂ ☿ lieblicher	3	5 8	6 52	18 Aeneas
samst	30 Eutropius	12	3 39	♈ 12	‡ ☁ sonnenschein,	3	5 7	6 53	19 Anicetus

ROUGHWOOD COLLECTION

A *Dutch Country German-language almanac for the year 1791. Maundy Thursday* (Gründonnerstag) *fell on April 21 that year.*

Pennsylvania German Society, meeting at York. Dr. A. Stapleton offered the following observation in a discussion of Dr. Fogel's paper:

In using the word superstition in connection with religion, I have no doubt that it occurs to us how closely the terms have been identified in the ages past, and it is easy to see how closely the two ideas were allied. I know that within our own family, over near the foot of the Blue Mountain in old Dutch Berks some fifty-one years ago, we had customs that we would never think of now, but in those days they were a part of our life. On Green Thursday we would just as reverently and sacredly gather the eggs that were laid that day for Easter morning breakfast, and if there were not enough eggs to go around father would divide the portion so that each would have a taste of the eggs. This was a part of our religious belief. You may call it superstition if you please, but it was a part of our religion and a custom that we followed regularly every year until I was a grown-up man.

Then father would take us out in the fields and we would go through the fields hunting for different herbs which were a cure for certain diseases. And in that practical way I learned what has never been taken away from me. After I was a high school boy I learned the technical part of botany, but the foundation was laid when I was a child. Snake root, sarsaparilla— all these things we gathered and they were just as much a part of our religion as we said our prayers, and we kept them to be used during the year for fever or any disease that we might be threatened with.

John F. Krebs, of near Jefferson, York County, told me on April 1, 1953, that the old-timers used to say if one did not eat an egg laid on Maundy Thursday, *du gaibsht en aisel* (you would become a mule).

There is a widely held folk belief in the Dutch Country that chickens hatched from eggs laid on Maundy Thursday will be speckled. The only deviation from this belief that I have ever collected comes from York County. An eighty-one-year-old woman told me in 1953 that her parents used to say that eggs set on Green Thursday would not hatch.

Since Maundy Thursday is in the heart of the growing season, there are a number of folk beliefs as to planting. A Mrs. Willis Burns, of York County, told me a number of years ago: "Cabbage seed must be sown on Maundy Thursday or else there will be no cabbage that year." A Mr. Troutman, a retired farmer living in Womelsdorf, told me in 1955 that he always planted his clover seed on Maundy Thursday. John Brendel, eighty, of Bowmansville, told me in 1955 that there was a belief in his area that one should mow the grass on Maundy Thursday. It would then stay nice and green that year and grow well, he said.

A Virginsville native, J. William Heffner, told me a number of years ago that his father used to put hay out[1] in the barnyard on the eve of Maundy Thursday; this he fed to the cows on Good Friday morning. The belief was that then *daita die kee net dick warra* (the cows would not become bloated).

GOOD FRIDAY

Up until recent decades—until the 1930s, say—Good Friday (*Karfreidawg*) was generally celebrated as a religious holiday throughout the Dutch Country. Farmers thought it sinful to engage in any farm labor other than the necessary chores. The women did not bake on this day, though Friday, of course, was the traditional baking day, nor did they sew or clean. The *Lehigh Valley Daily News* of March 28, 1872, described the manner of keeping Good Friday as follows:

To work on Good Friday, in the country, would be to depart from a custom that has prevailed in Lehigh, Northampton, Berks and other counties in this part of Pennsylvania from time immemorial; and would subject the innovator to the disfavor of his neighbors and the imputation of impurity.

Today this is all changed. It is only our "horse-and-buggy" Dutch farmers who any longer keep Good Friday as a holy day.

This change was brought about primarily as a result of industrialization. Factories and industries never considered Good Friday a holiday. Nor, in fact, did the rest of Protestant rural Pennsylvania, whether Quaker or Scotch-Irish Presbyterian by persuasion. A Reformed clergyman wrote in the *Reformirter Hausfreund* (published in Reading, Pennsylvania, on April 22, 1886): "A great part of our English-speaking neighbors hardly knows when Good Friday falls, whether it comes in Spring or in Fall."

It comes as quite a surprise, therefore, to learn that the Pennsylvania legislature by an act of April 10, 1869, established Good Friday as a legal holiday. How this was accomplished is not clear, for as the West Chester *Village Record* correctly observed on April 16, 1870: "this act was not called for by public opinion." And the Doylestown *Bucks County Intelligencer* of April 15, 1873, editorialized:

The general feeling among the people is quite adverse to the observance of Good Friday as a holiday, and nearly all of them would be glad to see the law repealed.

The act was on the books, but it was never honored in practice. The Lancaster *Intelligencer* of March 29, 1872, wrote:

Although this is Good Friday, and a legal holiday by legislative enactment, business of nearly every kind is being carried on as usual. The banks and a very few stores are closed, but the county offices and most other places are open.

Because the act of April 2, 1873, failed to mention it, the public was in doubt as to whether the law was still on the books. The Doylestown *Democrat* of April 7, 1874, wrote:

There being considerable doubt on the part of bankers, brokers, and other business men, as to whether Good Friday, according to the calendar, is a legal holiday, a telegram was sent to Attorney General Dimmick at Harrisburg, requesting his opinion in the matter. In response thereto the following telegram was received: "Sir, in reply to your telegram, I expressed the opinion last spring that Good Friday was a legal holiday. There has been no legislation since in relation thereto, and I remain of the same opinion, that Good Friday is a legal holiday.

The Good Friday act had, as I have said, no public support. Its only upholders were Pennsylvania's few Episcopalians, the Catholic element, then not yet important numerically, and the Pennsylvania Dutch. And so it passed into desuetude.

Even though the Pennsylvania Dutch element kept Good Friday as a holiday from the founding of the colony on, not everyone was altogether satisfied in the way it was being celebrated. This becomes apparent from a letter to the Allentown *Republikaner* of April 13, 1829. A Nazareth resident, very probably a Moravian, traveling to Sumneytown, wrote the paper:

I came by many taverns. Good Friday, the holy day on which the redeemer of the world suffered and died for us, how was it kept? The boys were pitching pennies, the girls were running around the community looking for fellows, the men were congregated in the inns talking about business deals and the women, they had gathered just to gossip. Very few spent their time in proper religious meditation.

Not all Pennsylvania Dutch kept the day as a holiday either. The Reading *Eagle* of March 27, 1880, brings this to the fore:

Kutztown. For a number of years, our merchants have been discussing the propriety of having their business establishments closed on Good Friday, but every time there was one among them who refused to close. The question has this year again been brought forward, and met with similar opposition by the same party. Yesterday morning, all the general stores were open as usual, when A. B. Urick who took considerable interest in the matter, visited every store, and by 8 o'clock in the forenoon, he had succeeded in inducing all to close up for the day, with the exception of J. S. Bieber, the oldest merchant in town, who was as sturdy as an oak of his age, and remarked that heretofore he had open on that day, and that he would not depart from his custom. The others kept closed and expect to do so on all legal holidays, hereafter. All the country stores, in this section of the county, were closed yesterday.

Ammon H. Bucher, of Manheim, Lancaster County, submitted an anecdote to me, showing that some of the Plain Dutch farmers of his county did not take the day too seriously either. Mr. Bucher wrote me:

A Good Friday hymn sheet printed in the German-language period.

Amos Sumpman, deceased, was hired when a boy with a wealthy farm family near Mt. Joy. Come Good Friday the farmer said to Amos, *"Hite iss Karfreidawg; mer schaffa nat hite. Du mawgsht der hinkel-roosht butza, es sheier-denn kaira, un die misht-wawga shmeera."* (Today's a holiday; we'll not do any work today. But you might clean the chicken roost, sweep the threshing floor, and grease the manure wagon.) These jobs took Amos the greater part of the day. Well, Amos was extremely irked, and he left the farm before another Good Friday came around. But every year afterwards on Good Friday Amos would say to all around him, "*Ya, hite iss Karfreidawg; mer schaffa nat hite, yusht der hinkel-roosht butza, sheier-denn kaira, die wawga shmeera.*" And he would end by saying "*Fer-dammta Grishta!*" (Damn Christians!)

The Amish, who hold to old ways more so than other groups among the Pennsylvania Dutch, observe two fast days a year, Good Friday and St. Michael's Day. One J. D. Z., writing in the *Reformirter Hausfreund* of April 22, 1886, in connection with the early manner of keeping Good Friday among the Reformed fathers, had this to say: "One fasted on Good Friday, often to sunset before one took any food."

The folklore centering around Good Friday in the Pennsylvania Dutch Country concerns (1) work taboos—farm and household; (2) the eggs laid on this day; (3) sympathetic folk cures; and (4) weather prognostication.

Morris A. Frantz, of Reading, told me a number of years ago of a farmer in upper Berks County who began sowing a field in oats on Good Friday and finished on Saturday. The oats sown on Good Friday grew only eight inches high and did not yield any harvest at all. However, the oats in the same field that was sown on the Saturday following Good Friday yielded one of the best crops the farmer ever had.

There is one important exception to this folk belief that no farm work should be undertaken on this day: Good Friday morning was the universally prescribed time to sow clover seed. However, the sowing had to be completed in the forenoon. To have worked on into the afternoon of Good Friday would have been considered inadmissible.

The women did not bake, sew, or sweep (clean) the house on this day of Holy Week. Mrs. Harry Senft, of Jefferson, York County, told me of a folk belief in her family to the effect that if you bake on Good Friday you either bake someone into the family, or you bake someone out of it: *Du backsht ains in die familya adder ains aus da familya.* Either there would be an addition in the family, a baby, or there would be a death. Mrs. Cora Snyder of the same place put it this way: "*Mer backt ains raus adder mer backt ains naus.*"

Mrs. John Beaver, of Kratzerville, Snyder County, told me the women in her section say you should not bake (*mer sott net ins mail gay*) on Good Friday; if you did, your cabbage would mildew. Mrs. Thomas Shaffer, of Meiserville, says the folk belief in her area was as follows: If you bake on Good Friday the bread will be no good all year long. (*Es broat iss no darrich s gons yawr net gute.*)

The reason there are so many baking taboos is, of course, that Friday formerly was baking day—the day when the week's supply of bread, pies, and cakes was baked. There is no washing lore concerning this day, obviously because Friday is not a wash day. There is, however, a sewing taboo, though it is not nearly so strict as that on Ascension Day.

Mrs. John Beaver told me of the folk belief that you will be bothered with ants in your house if you sweep the house on Good Friday. On the other hand, Dr. Ezra Grumbine, in an article "Folk-lore and Superstitious Beliefs of Lebanon County" (*Proceedings of the Lebanon County Historical Society*, volume 3, page 285), wrote:

A propitious season for cleaning cupboards and closets was on Good Friday, and there are still many housewives who believe that this practice will keep moths and other pests out of the house.

And Dr. Edwin M. Fogel, in his volume on the superstitions of the Pennsylvania Dutch (page 251), collected this belief: Sweeping all the rooms on Good Friday and burning the sweepings brings good luck.

Strangely enough, in view of the work taboos on Good Friday, there was no taboo in planting seeds, though it was considered wrong to work in the garden. One was not to work in the garden between Good Friday and Easter because Jesus was buried in the earth those three days.

In Lancaster and York counties I repeatedly heard that Good Friday was the time to plant cabbage seed. The Lancaster *Intelligencer* of April 10, 1868, observed:

There is a general belief that cabbage seed sown on Good Friday will produce stronger and hardier plants than when sown on any other day.

Dr. Fogel, in his volume on superstitions, has recorded a couple of folk beliefs to the effect that if you sow flower seeds on Good Friday, the plants will bear variegated flowers. Though I have never myself collected this folk belief orally, I have come upon it in the newspaper press of the Pennsylvania Dutch Country. The York *True Democrat* of March 23, 1869, wrote:

Sow your annual flower seeds on Friday next. That will be Good Friday and by a well observed usage it is the time selected. There may not be anything particularly virtuous in the day, but the testimony of the world is that flower seed sown at that time grows well and produces a beautiful crop. It is at least worthy of a trial.

The last sentence expresses the Pennsylvania Dutch philosophy *Wann's nix batt, schatt's nix.* (If it does not help, it won't do any harm.)

Generally, Good Friday eggs, if eaten either on Good Friday itself or if kept for Easter breakfast, are believed to secure good health and good luck to the eater. Mrs. Charles Dry, of near Fredericksville, Berks County, told me a number of years ago that her husband's aunts used to come all the way from Wyomissing on Good Friday to the family farm to make absolutely sure that they would have Good Friday eggs to eat for Easter breakfast.

Eggs laid on Good Friday are used in sympathetic (magic) folk medicine. I shall list here but a few of the many instances of their use I have collected through the past ten years. Mrs. Cora Snyder, of whom there was a mention above, told me she suffered from a goiter many years ago. All medical aid proved ineffectual. So she followed this folk cure: She rubbed an egg laid on Good Friday over her goiter and hid the egg behind the chimney in the attic. She said her goiter went away.

William Reinert, of Berks County, told me if you rub a Good Friday egg around a baby's mouth, the baby will not suffer from a sore mouth. He said, too, one should not sell Good Friday eggs; "*du daitsht dei glick ferkawfa*" (you would sell your good luck).

Marie Master, of near Mt. Pleasant Mills, Snyder County, tells me one of her neighbors said an egg laid by a black hen (must be black all over) on Good Friday was effective in removing a birthmark. If the birthmark was rubbed with such an egg, the mark would end up at one's navel, she said.

I picked up a very interesting folk belief concerning eggs laid on Good Friday in the *Grubba Karrich* area of Snyder County. I visited with Maggie Long. She said both her father and mother used to powwow. Her father was David Schreiber and her mother Maria McBride, a native of Ireland. Mrs. Long's father used to take two eggs laid on Good Friday, place them in a can, and put them in a drawer where they would not be disturbed. Lightning would not strike the house if this was done each year was the folk belief. Agnes Wendt, of near Hoffer, told me it was her father's practice to take an egg laid on Good Friday and place it in the attic under a crock, so that nothing could get at it. There was the folk belief that then lightning would not strike that house.

In Palmerton, Carbon County, I collected my favorite Good Friday folk belief. A Mrs. Benjamin Bachman told me February 28, 1959, of the custom of saving the egg shells of eggs laid and eaten on Good Friday (for health). The egg shells were kept until Easter and on Easter morning they filled the egg shell with water and drank it from the shell. This, I understood, is done to this day. The purpose is to assure oneself good health for the coming year.

Throughout the Pennsylvania Dutch Country I have come upon the folk belief that eggs laid on Good Friday are particularly good for setting purposes. The chicks hatched from these eggs, it is believed, will become *schechicha* (speckled) chickens.

One of the best studies to date on the folk culture of the Pennsylvania Dutch Country is Thomas R. Brendle and Claude W. Unger's *Folk Medicine of the Pennsylvania Germans*, published by the Pennsylvania German Society in 1935. Much of the material in this volume was gathered from original manuscript sources, most of them translated from the German language of early Pennsylvania. Four of the cures, all of them sympathetic (magic) cures, are in some way connected with Good Friday. They follow:

1) How to get wound wood (page 75):

To cut wound wood. Go out and hunt a small ash tree. On Good Friday, before sunrise, take a sharp hatchet or axe and cut off a branch or the whole tree with three strokes—it is to be noted that if the tree does not fall after three strokes the wood is useless. After cutting the wood rightly let it lie until the sun is risen and shines upon it, then cut the wood up into small pieces and you have the true wound wood. Preserve it well. If you should hack, stab, cut, or pinch yourself, so that the flow of blood is not easily stilled, lay the wood upon the wound so that the wood becomes warm and the wound will heal without festering. If your horse has a swelling lay the wood upon the swelling and make three crosses upon it.

2) For toothache (pages 117–118):

Cut the nails from hands and feet on a Friday in the decrease of the moon and wrap them in a white paper, then go on the north side of a building, bury the paper under the eaves and *verrichte deine*

Nothdurft dahin [defecate on it]. If you do this three times a year you can keep away toothaches as long as you live. If the decrease of the moon comes on Good Friday it will help for a whole year.

3) For sweeny (pages 148–149):

On Good Friday, after 12 o'clock, go, without speaking and unbeshrewed, to an aspen tree and cut off a piece of wood, saw from it pieces the length of match sticks and also cut the pieces as thin as match sticks (*Schwefel holzer*). Set up the pieces on the stove, like a house, set them afire so that they will burn to coals, take off this coal and put in a rag taken from the arm of a man's shirt, and hang around the afflicted part.

4) For a rupture (page 187):

On Good Friday, before sunrise, go to a healthy apple tree, cut a peg out of the wood of the tree, bore a hole in the tree on the morning side and knock in the plug with three strokes, and in the striking say, I knock in this plug that Mr. or Mrs. (*dem oder der*) N. N.'s rupture will grow herein X X X.

Rev. Thomas R. Brendle of Egypt, Lehigh County, the dean of Pennsylvania Dutch folklorists, wrote in an article in the *Pennsylvania Dutchman* of November 15, 1951: The weather on Good Friday is expected to be rough and raw, a manifestation of divine wrath." In Lancaster and Lebanon counties I have frequently come upon this bit of weather lore: *Wann die kawr-woch schay iss, iss die naigsht-woch weesht un iss die kawr-woch weesht, iss die naigsht woch schay.* (If the weather during Passion Week is beautiful, the following week's weather will be ugly. And if Passion Week is an ugly week, the following week will be a nice one.)

The general belief is that if it rains on Good Friday, *badda die raiya nix, s dutt grawd uffdrickla.* (The rains will be of no avail, because they will immediately dry up.)

I want to list two more interesting weather prognostications: (1) There will be rain on Good Friday, even if only three drops; and (2) the sun will never shine clearly before nine o'clock in the morning on Good Friday.

EASTER LORE

The word *Easter*—apart from its religious implications—calls four things to mind: colored eggs; the egg-laying rabbit; spring bonnets;[1] and one widely held bit of weather lore, that a white Christmas foretells a green Easter, or a white Easter, a green Christmas.

In the Dutch Country the weeks immediately preceding Easter were given over to seeing to it that there was a plentiful supply of eggs on hand for the sundry uses of the Easter holiday.

The Lebanon *Daily Times* of April 8, 1881, described this custom:

It has been the custom for very many years among the farmers' children and hired hands on farms to collect and hide away somewhere in the barn nearly all the hens' eggs that are laid within a month or six weeks before Easter. In some parts of the country this custom prevails as much as it did half a century ago. Where chickens are it is not an unusual thing for the employees on a farm to hide in boxes hid in the hay 100 dozens or more, while the farmer's wife is put to inconvenience in cooking and baking on account of the scarcity of eggs. The accumulated eggs are generally brought from the hiding places on Good Friday and taken in the house to astonish the heads of the family, and eggs suddenly become very plentiful. Many of them are then boiled and colored and eaten during the Easter festival.

Professor Joseph H. Dubbs (1838–1910), one of our early folklorists, described the custom of hiding eggs at Easter time in his reminiscences:

Boys sometimes hid away eggs, in order that they might have a large number to bring into the house on Easter morning. Aided by a hired man, I was engaged in an affair of this kind, and was sorry for it afterwards. For weeks we hid eggs in a safe place

[in] the haymow, taking one or two to the house occasionally to keep up appearances. At that time eggs were scarce, and those we hid might have been sold at a high price; but when on Easter morning we brought in a large basketful they had become a "drug in the market." My mother was naturally displeased, and I determined never to play such a trick again.

The Reverend C. S. Albert, a Pennsylvania native, tells, too, of the custom of hiding eggs before the holiday (*St. Mark's Quarterly*, April 1893):

The Easter of boyhood spent in a village community has few memories characteristic of the great festival. The boys thought Easter was chiefly memorable for eggs. For some time before the day, they hid away the eggs they found in the nests in the fragrant hay. The good housewife was sorely puzzled by the sudden failure of the hens to lay. The boys kept quiet as she scolded the faithful fowls, and looked wisely at each other. The day before Easter they trooped in with a great basketful of eggs clamoring to have them boiled hard and colored. It was the pride of each boy to have as many eggs as he could get, and on Easter to eat as many as he could, ending up usually with the doctor.

So great was the enthusiasm on the part of youth to secure an adequate number of eggs that some of them—poor city boys—even resorted to stealing them. Such a case is described in the York *True Democrat* of April 15, 1873:

Egg Thieves. A party of boys from York went a short distance to the country last week, to lay in a supply of Easter eggs, by stealing. They succeeded in securing a good supply, as the premises upon which they made the raid were full of well filled nests. After they had left the place one of the crowd missed a very desirable mouth organ, which he had lost while absorbed in making the search for eggs, and he was [so] anxious to get it

A photograph—taken by H. Winslow Fegley around the turn of the century—of a woman in the Pennsylvania Dutch Country preparing to dye Easter eggs with onion skins.

back again, that a day or so afterwards he went and made inquiry about the much prized treasure. He put in a plea that he had been with a crowd of boys who stole the eggs, but that they were rotten, and that he didn't take any himself. He also offered three eggs for the mouth organ which had been found near one of the nests, on the discovery of the robbery, but he was obliged to leave without it.

TRADITIONAL MANNER OF COLORING EGGS

The traditional way to color Easter eggs in the Pennsylvania Dutch Country is to boil them in onion skins. This is done usually on the Saturday before Easter, at a time when the children are not about. Many families did not, and do not now, use commercial dyes because they fear if the shell cracked and the child ate the egg, there might be a danger of being poisoned.

There are less common ways to color Easter eggs, but the manner is still traditional. Alder catkins (*alla-hecka schwens*) and hickory bark dye them yellow; madder root (*grabb*) makes them a light red. Green wheat or rye were also occasionally used. Coffee and walnut hulls dyed them brown. Another old-time method was to wrap the eggs tightly in flowered calico and boil them thus. The colored patterns were faithfully transferred to the egg. Mrs. Stella Burkhart, of near Red Run, Lancaster County, told me that the "calico eggs" were cooked in soap lye (*saifa-lawk*) to bring out the color, but that these eggs were just "for nice" and not for eating.

Cardboard boxes were used as containers for gifts of elaborately decorated scratch-carved Easter eggs.

The Lebanon *Daily Times* of April 16, 1892, refers to the manner of dyeing calico eggs:

An old-fashioned method was to tie each egg in a piece of figured chintz or calico which would leave its print on the egg after it had been exposed to the action of boiling water. . . . To color eggs with an original design, an old time method was to trace figures upon the shells of raw eggs with a bit of hard tallow candle, thus covering the part of the shell which was to remain white, and then to put the eggs in boiling dye-water.

On the humorous side is a brief note in the Reading *Berks and Schuylkill Journal* of April 3, 1875: "Easton should encourage Spelling Skules. Among her announcements are 'Kalliko-Kollered Egs for Easter.'"

BINSA-GRAWS EASTER EGGS

Of all early traditional modes of decorating Easter eggs in the Dutch Country, to me the most interesting I have unearthed is the one using the pith of *binsa-graws*, a meadow rush, growing generally where the soil is quite damp.

Norman Smith,[2] of Lenhartsville, Berks County, was the first person to call my attention to this style of egg decorating. He has an old *binsa-graws* Easter egg among his collection of family heirlooms.

The manner of making *binsa-graws* Easter eggs is as follows: One forces a goodly quantity of pith from rush, by means of a match stick or some other instrument of like size. A flour paste is prepared and the pith, woolly in appearance and texture, is then wound around the egg in coils. (The eggs are always blown beforehand for purposes of easier handling.) After the egg shell is completely covered with the rush, small pieces of colorful calico are cut out in interesting shapes and pasted on the rush-covered surface of the egg.

Mrs. Laura Huyett, of near Narvon, Lancaster County, has revived this mode of decorating Easter eggs on a large scale, first at the 1958 Pennsylvania

An old Amish Easter egg. An Amish woman pasted cloths of various designs on the egg and outlined the spaces separating the pieces of cloth with strands of binsa-graws pith.

Dutch Folk Festival at Kutztown. Mrs. Huyett was taught the art by Mrs. Viola Miller of the staff of the Pennsylvania Folklife Society, who made several experimental eggs at my suggestion for the first time in the spring of 1958. The link in the whole revival was an elderly woman in Myerstown, Lebanon County, who remembered how the *binsa-graws* pith was gathered and used in her childhood home to decorate, in flower clusters, the base of the old-time coal oil lights.

In searching the Dutch Country for additional information about *binsa-graws* eggs, Mrs. Huyett has come upon a variant of this style of decoration in

Top left: Laura Huyett demonstrating the removal of pith from the binsa-graws. *Top right: The* binsa-graws *pith is pasted in coils around the egg. Bottom right: Calico, in interesting designs, is then pasted on the egg.*

use among the Lancaster County Amish women long years ago. Instead of covering the egg completely with the pith of the rush before the calico is attached, the Amish method was to paste the cloth directly on the egg in interesting layouts. The spaces separating the various pieces of cloth were then outlined with single strands of *binsa-graws* pith.

EASTER EGG BIRDS

One of the decorative uses of eggs at Easter time in the Dutch Country in years gone by was to make Easter egg birds, sometimes also referred to as Easter birds. I have come upon this practice only in

An Easter egg tree, cotton-wrapped and decorated with colorful binsa-graws *Easter eggs.*

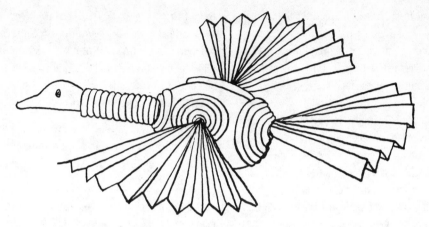

Ostervogel (Easter bird) from the Odenwald in Hessen. The eggshell and neck are wound with strands of binsa-graws. *From the* Schweizerisches Archiv für Volkskunde *(1957)*.

Adams County. At this juncture I shall now reproduce a short article I wrote on this subject in the *Pennsylvania Dutchman* of May 15, 1950.

The most interesting people of my acquaintance, I met "on" cemeteries and John Staub, of near Hampton, Adams County, is no exception.

It was some twelve years ago. At the time I was following the grand sport of epitaph hunting at Trappe, the God's Acre where sleeps the father of the Lutheran church of America.

And it was near the grave of patriarch Henry Melchior Muhlenberg that I ran into John. He, I learned, had come all the way from Adams County in an attempt to straighten out one of his lines—the Shracks.

We struck up a conversation. (I was a fledgling philologist at the time, working on the Pennsylvania Dutch dialect.) And John Staub it was who that day first called my attention to the fact that there are parts of Adams County where the dialect is spoken. Somehow I managed then and there to get myself invited to Hampton—to hear Adams County Dutch and, what proved even more fascinating, to see a house full of antiques, untouched since the days of the Civil War.

There are many memories of that visit—the evening spent with hermit Willis Hartman who was the finest storyteller and folksong singer of Adams County; the ham and egg breakfast at the Daniel Hinkle's who lodged and fed me; the visit in Abbottstown with Charlie Hafer, the only dialect writer I know of who hailed from Adams County; and best of all—the *oschter-feggel* (Easter birds) or egg birds.

The Easter bird is a chapter in itself. From the ceiling of the old log house, unchanged as I said, since before the Civil War, hung several dozen Easter birds, "flying" in the breeze of an open window.

But lest I get ahead of myself. Do you know what I mean by an *oschter-foggel* (easter bird) or egg bird? Simple. Our Pennsylvania Dutch great-grandparents took a dyed egg, blew it and made four holes in it—one for the head; two, in the sides, for wings; and lastly, one for the tail. And these egg birds served as a decoration in the living rooms of long ago.

Aging Mrs. J. C. Leinart, of near Hampton, told me just this past Sunday that in Spring when she was a little girl, when the stove was taken down in the living room, her mother always covered the stovepipe hole with half a dozen or so of the gaily colored egg birds. Though it's been fifty years since Mrs. Leinart saw her last egg bird, she tells me she can still see them in her memory, waving in the summer's breeze.

I didn't get back to Hampton and John Staub's again for some twelve years—not until just this past Sunday.

And the motive? In preparing an article for the DUTCH-MAN on Easter egg trees I paged anew through the volumes on German folklore in my library and in a lovely little booklet on German folk art by Siegfried Lehman (1943) I came upon an article, with an accompanying picture, of an "Ostervogel" or Easter bird or egg bird.

My memories stirred. I recalled the pleasant days of a decade ago. And I set out for Hampton and John Staub's.

Knowing John as I did, I knew if he were alive, the old log house would be unchanged. And unchanged it was in the main. The only difference was that John's hair had turned a deeper gray and that the Easter birds had been moved from downstairs to upstairs. And John gave me three of them to take along home. All of them (imagine it!) had hung in the old log house since before the Civil War.

Elated, I brought them back to the Folklore Center. But as I climbed the stairs to my third floor office, the old, hand-woven thread broke and all three of the Easter birds fell to the floor. And there they lay, crushed through my great carelessness—broken, wings and all, after having "flown" in the breezes of well-nigh a hundred years.

EARLY DOCUMENTATION

References to Easter eggs—even references to the Easter festival itself—in the early Pennsylvania newspapers are all but nonexistent. In the German-language press of Pennsylvania, the very first mention I have been able to find of Easter eggs is in the Lancaster *Volksfreund* of April 13, 1824:

Eine sehr allgemeine Sitte schenkt bey uns zu Ostern den Kindern bunt gemalte Eyer. (A general custom with us is that of presenting children at Easter gaily colored eggs.)

That some of the early Pennsylvania Dutch were not always in sympathy with the custom of presenting Easter eggs is apparent from an item in the Allentown *Unabhaengiger Republikaner* of April 10, 1828:

Ostereyer. Wir bemerken mit Vergnuegen dass dieses Jahr weniger von diesen Giftballen unter unsern Kindern zu sehen waren als jemals. Die Eltern verdienen Lob dass sie dem einfaeltigen und gefaehrlichen Gebrauch ein End machen. (Easter eggs. We note with pleasure that fewer of these poison balls were to be seen among our children than ever before. Parents deserve praise that they have put an end to this stupid and dangerous custom.)

The best early reference to secular Easter customs—though completely denunciatory—is a letter to the editor of the Allentown *Republikaner* of April 23, 1829:

Permit me a bit of space in your beloved paper for a few comments about the observance of the so-called holidays. The Easter holidays have passed and that leads me to write this little article. I was on a journey from Nazareth to Sumneytown and on my way I passed many taverns.

And Easter Sunday! Nowhere did I see on my journey the celebration of any Easter services—everywhere however colored eggs that the rabbit had laid! The little ones were picking eggs; the old folks were scratching tulips on the eggs. The young lads ran around to invite their sweethearts to the frolic and the maidens were looking for their beaus, if the latter were not looking for them. No one was giving thought to this holy day of the resurrection of Jesus. And is this the way to observe a holiday? I had rather be busied with making fences on such a day than to celebrate it in this fashion.

COMMERCIALIZATION

In the second half of the nineteenth century the drug store and the local confectioner entered the Easter picture. Commercial dyes began to be marketed, replacing in large part the old-time home methods of decorating the Easter eggs. And the confectionery shop started dyeing the eggs in quantity, thus "saving" mother—as they said in their newspaper advertising—the "drudgery" and all the mess of coloring the Easter eggs. Also, the candy eggs began in part to replace the hens' eggs about this time. This volume, concerned exclusively with folk practices, will not present the story of the gradual commercialization of the Easter festival.

I shall cite but one instance of the type of advice in coloring Easter eggs which the newspapers began to pass to their readers in the transitional period from the use of all home dyes to commercial dyes. The York *Evening Dispatch* of March 26, 1880, wrote:

Eggs may be colored beautifully and safely by dipping them in solutions of the analine colors: for dark red, in logwood; for blue, in indigo; for brown or purple, first in indigo and then in logwood or madder; for yellow, in gamboge; for green, first in gamboge and then in indigo. Stripes of different colors may be made by wrapping rubber bands around parts of the egg and coloring the rest; then drying and changing the bands on to colored parts, and then coloring the fresh places; various devices may be made by using broad bands cut like stencil plates, or the bands may be made around the eggs both ways, and so be made to form checks.

Coloring Easter eggs passed from being an art to a science. The Lebanon *Daily Times* of April 16, 1881, brings this to the fore:

Mr. C. R. Fisher, the North Ninth street dyer, is just now kept busy coloring Easter eggs, which he does in a scientific manner. For five cents a dozen he changes the natural color into purple, yellow, and red, or red, white, and blue, the effect of the latter combination being very pleasing. Judging from samples shown us, it is certainly the part of wisdom to take your hard-boiled eggs to his dyeing establishment for coloring. The sum charged is trifling compared to the trouble saved.

As said, candy Easter eggs began to replace ordinary eggs. Dr. B. Frank Witmer, in an article[3] in the Lancaster *Sunday News* of April 1, 1934, wrote that Joseph Huber and Joseph Royer, two Lancaster confectioners, invented the "Easter candy symbol." A representative early Easter candy advertisement follows from the York *Daily* of April 15, 1876:

P. C. Wiest's Easter Bulletin. Grand Display of Fancy Easter Eggs, from 5 cents per piece up. The first goods of the kind ever kept in York. Don't fail to call and see them.

This was the time, too, when the artificial eggs began to appear in the stores and confectionery shops. One of the earliest references in the press I have to them is from the Lebanon *Advertiser* of April 1, 1874:

We were shown the other day a beautiful glass Easter Egg, by Mr. Peter L. Zimmerman, which is on exhibition at his Notion and Trimming Store, on South 8th street. In looking into the glass the eye will behold a beautiful Easter scenery. It is a curiosity, and is looked at by all who pass their store.

EGG-EATING CONTESTS

It has been a custom in the Dutch Country from time immemorial to eat a goodly number of eggs, usually hard-boiled ones, for breakfast on Easter morning. There are many tales of contests to determine who could eat the greatest number of eggs at this time. The largest number I heard of being consumed in such a challenge was eighteen goose eggs. Alvin Wissler, of near Lancaster, recently recalled:

Men used to challenge each other as to who could eat the most eggs. When I was a boy my father challenged the hired man one Easter morning as to who could eat the most. It ended up that my father ate fourteen eggs and the hired man twelve.

The Reverend C. S. Albert, in an article in *St. Mark's Quarterly* for April 1893, alludes to this lore:

I recall the fearful delight with which I listened to a story of my father concerning a certain woman, who having heard of persons eating twelve hard-boiled eggs, determined to try it. After the doctor had pulled her through an illness of which she nearly died, she said, "I often heerd of people eating twelve eggs and I thought I'd try. I ate eleven but I stuck on the yaller of the twelfth. But, oh! I was so sick; I never want to try it again." Perhaps the whole story was a wise scheme on the part of father to keep the boys from gorging themselves. Certainly it made us cautious.

The editor of the West Chester *Village Record* (April 7, 1874) made a humorous allusion to this custom of consuming large numbers of eggs at Easter breakfast:

The capability for eating eggs is always taxed to the utmost on Easter Sunday, for in order to properly celebrate the day one must eat as many eggs as possible. We did our best and ate *one.*

Juvenile champion, no doubt, for all time was the six-year-old Columbia lad who, according to the York *Dispatch* of April 23, 1878,

took it into his head to properly celebrate Easter, so while his mother was at church on Sunday, he proceeded to devour nine hard boiled eggs, two sugar eggs, an orange, and finished up with a piece of lemon custard.

The Carlisle *Herald* of April 16, 1874, reported: "A Lancaster county man is said to have eaten 56 eggs on Easter Monday. We don't believe it." And nor do we, but at least we have an idea—an excellent one, too—of the type of tall tales that must have circulated about the prowess of champion Easter egg eaters in the Dutchland of a century ago.

PICKING EASTER EGGS

We come now to the universal Easter pastime—picking eggs. Children tested the strength of the shells by striking the end of the eggs together. It was the rule among the youngsters that the egg that was broken fell a prize to the one that broke it. In rural communities, where there were fewer occasions to pick eggs than in the towns and cities, the children sometimes picked the eggs on their own foreheads.

The G. A. Berner folklore manuscript at the Pottsville Public Library gives us a good description of this game:

An egg-picking illustration from Horne's Pennsylvania German Manual (*third edition, Allentown, 1905*).

A sport the boys used to have a couple of weeks before Easter and that was the fun of "Picking Eggs." A couple of weeks before Easter you could hear the boys cry "Pick Eggs." The boys hearing the cry would engage the challenger and would produce his egg for picking point for point and butt for butt. The boy whose egg was broken surrendered his egg and the winner was ready for the next one. Some of the boys would gather up quite a few eggs that way and take them home, especially when he would use a guinea egg or one especially doctored up for the winning.

Below the reader will find the major literature on picking eggs in the Dutch Country.

From the Easton *Argus* of April 20, 1854.
We observed a considerable excitement among the juveniles in regard to the quality of eggs, which were in demand for Easter-cracking. The "Hard Shells" were triumphant, and the "Softs" were down.

From the Norristown *Montgomery Watchman* of March 25, 1856.
Eggs had to suffer yesterday, but "nary" one did we see as of old in a youngster's hand, bantering to fights. Alas! that all the sports of by-gone days are past. Young America has taken to cigars, tight breeches and big cravats, instead of keeping alive the time-honored custom of fighting colored wooden eggs against the

fruit of the chicken. Truly, the human race is degenerating and the country is in danger.

From the Easton *Daily Express* of April 3, 1858.
Groups of boys may be seen in the street, earnestly engaged in "picking," while such exclamations as "my pick against your pick," and "my butt against your butt," are heard wherever these gatherings are.

From the *Lutheran and Missionary* of April 13, 1865. [There follows the major part of a literary piece, called "Fred's Easter Egg," written by N. A. M. E. of Harrisburg.]
A boy knocked at the side door, and with his hands pocketed, whistled away the time which elapsed before the door was opened. I had a fine opportunity of scanning him, which I improved, as there was that about him which does, or should pertain to every healthy, wideawake boy of ten years, an exuberance of life and joy, of which his sparkling brown eyes, shrill whistle, and the restless patting of his feet were but three tiny outlets.

Soon a lady answered his rap. Off went his black cap, and the hearty "Good-morning, aunty," wore a smile of real welcome, which the most studied politeness of after years may fail to obtain for him.

"Well, Fred; come in, won't you?"

"No, aunty, I just want to ask you something. You know your speckled hen, old Jerusha."

"Yes! What of her?"

"Don't she lay every day now?"

"I think so."

"Them kind of hens are good layers."

Aunty's lips twicked knowingly at this bit of gratuitous information, but said nothing. Fred continued.

"Easter's most here. My! but some of the boys have lots of eggs. Jim Duncan's aunt Christie gave him three dozen."

"And you want me to follow her example, Fred; is that it?"

"No, aunty; I wouldn't be bothered with so many at once; but I thought maybe you'd give me *one* of Jerusha's eggs."

"Why, what a moderate request. Of course I will," And directly a dark yellow egg lay in his hand.

"This will fetch 'em," said Fred, tapping it against his teeth to test its firmness; then producing from his jacket pocket the egg of a Guinea fowl, he laid both in his hand as admiringly as the Duke of Brunswick would two diamonds of similar size.

"They are splendid fellows, aunty. I wish there was some way of making them harder yet."

"Then you couldn't break them, Fred!"

"Break them, aunty!" said Fred, looking up in surprise. "Why, you're gr——. Oh, I didn't mean that, (clapping his hand to his mouth,) but you're so funny. Why, I swapped a knife, that had one good blade in it, just for this little Guinea egg, because the shell is so tough and hard. There aren't two more like it in town."

"Do you intend to swallow them whole, Fred, since they are not to be broken?"

He frowned a little, impatiently, at his aunt's pretended ignorance, maybe, but answered respectfully, "No, ma'am, I want them for pickers. I bet I can win my cap full with these fellows."

"But I'll save you that trouble, dear. I'll give you a dozen for nothing."

"La, aunt, it won't be any *trouble* with these. I'll just win them as easy as a pin."

"Why do you want to win them, when I can give them to you?"

"Oh, just for the *fun* of it."

"Do you think it is fun for those boys who lose their eggs to you?"

"That's their look-out, not mine."

"Suppose, by some accident, *you* lose, then where's the fun?"

Fred was getting a little fidgety. He didn't like such close questioning, but answered, carelessly, "I wouldn't care a bit."

"Then, if you don't care, why have you gone to such pains to get those unusually hard eggs?"

"Because . . . why," but the answer wouldn't come . . .

[The rest of the piece is devoted to the aunt teaching the boy a moral lesson.]

From the Harrisburg *Daily Telegraph* of April 20, 1867.
The old custom of eating eggs on this occasion is universally observed in this country. Easter would not be Easter without a

bountiful supply of eggs. The children must have "hard-boiled" colored eggs, which they throw about, or play "pipp" with their little neighbors.

From the Allentown *Lehigh Valley Daily News* of April 13, 1868.

Egg picking prevailed to a great extent yesterday. In all parts of the city juveniles could be seen with their favorite eggs in hand challenging whoever might come along to try their metal. Would it not have been better for these young folks to postpone their games until after Sabbath day? Certainly to-day [Easter Monday] would have been more appropriate—if such proceedings are to take place at all.

From the York *True Democrat* of March 30, 1869.

Easter Sunday and Monday passed with us, this year, in rather a quiet and orderly manner. There were not any marked or notorious excesses that came under our notice. The juveniles had their usual privilege and enjoyment of shouting out their *nary eggs* along the streets, and hundreds of them were duly picked and broken.

From the Lebanon *Courier* of April 1, 1869.

Easter was duly celebrated by the younger portion of our community, and the traditional Easter egg was decidedly prevalent. The pavements on all sides were strewn with shells, and everywhere you could see the "young 'uns" bantering each other to "peck," some of the more mischievous and tricky having eggs of China, with which they could "sweep the field," while others would have eggs innocent of hot water, which they would smash into their opponent's hands, to the utter consternation of the holder-up.

From the Carlisle *Herald* of March 28, 1871.

Sabbath next will be Easter. Already the shouts of Young America, "hold her up," greet the ear on every hand, as they are eager to "pick" eggs with their companions.

From the Easton *Evening Free Press* of April 8, 1871.

To many older readers they [the Easter holidays] bring a reminiscence of youthful days, when whole towns broke out by spontaneity into a hen furore, and people went about cracking hard boiled eggs with each other, and predicting upon the result all manner of future benefits and good auguries.

From the Carlisle *Herald* of April 17, 1873.

Easter. Notwithstanding the day, we observed Young America busily "picking" eggs,—even some boys who were on their way to Sabbath School.

From the Pottsville *Miners' Journal* of April 17, 1876.

The noble and elevating pastime of picking eggs was a good deal indulged in here on Saturday—even by adults.

From the Reading *Eagle* of April 3, 1877.

Kutztown news item: On Sunday morning some made it a business to go from one friend to the other and collect an "oster haas" from each of them. In picking the eggs, by knocking two against each other, the one's egg that breaks first being given to the other. The cunning chap who had provided himself with a wooden colored one took many prizes.

From the Lebanon *Daily Times* of April 18, 1881.

Easter Monday. Picking eggs will take the place of ball and bat among the boys to-day.

From *St. Mark's Quarterly* of April 1893.

Picking eggs was great sport then as now, and every boy sought for a "bully" one that might smash the eggs of all the others. The tough shell often did go through a half-dozen picks, but the successive pickings weakened it so that at length it fell a victim to some other "bully." It was a hard test of virtue to refuse to pick eggs on Sunday and the conscientious boy wondered at the stupidity that made Easter and Sunday come together. He preferred a shifting day like that of Christmas.

From the York *Age* of March 24, 1894.

Picking Eggs for Keeps. The old custom of "picking eggs for keeps" at Easter seems to have died out. In the olden times the boys went around the streets at this season of the year with one or more eggs in their pockets, ready for a pick with any chap that came along. Guinea eggs bleached with a bath in vinegar, or chicken eggs filled with rosin, were used by some of the boy sharpers. These fellows would go round the streets yelling "airy egg," and succeeded in winning many eggs from the uninitiated and verdant.

EASTER EGGS AS SUNDAY SCHOOL GIFTS

Somewhere along the turn of the middle of the nineteenth century the Easter egg, like Santa Claus, invaded the Sunday school.

At the close of Sunday school Easter festivals—sometimes held on Easter Monday—the scholars were each presented with a gift of Easter eggs. The earliest evidence I have been able to locate to this practice is for the year 1866. A brief article in the York *True Democrat* of April 10, 1866, said:

Easter Festival. A pleasant gathering of the teachers, church members and Sabbath School children, was held in the lecture room of Rev. Mr. Baum's church, in South Beaver St., on the afternoon of Easter Monday. The ladies connected with the congregation, and some of the liberal minded gentlemen of the church, laid in an abundant supply of the good things of the season, cakes, oranges, eggs, &c., which were distributed among the children, and also partaken of by some of the larger persons present.

The earliest reference for Western Pennsylvania that I located is from the year 1867. The Bedford *Gazette* of April 26, 1867, alluding to the Sunday school festival of St. James Episcopal Church (the meeting was held in the court house), wrote:

The Rector, Rev. M. Barrow, made a short but beautiful address, after which he presented an Easter egg, beautifully colored and decorated, and a handsome bouquet of spring flowers, to each member of the Sunday School.

Not without humor was the coming of the Easter festival into those churches which had been vehemently opposed to the celebration of Easter up to the last years of the nineteenth century. Such an instance is the account of the first Sunday school festival in 1880 in the Methodist church at Bristol, Bucks County (from the Doylestown *Democrat* of April 6, 1880):

It was the first time in the history of the school that a special Easter service was held. It would have made our old-fashioned Methodists open their eyes in wonder could they have been present. The pulpit was removed and a stage built, upon which, at the back, a pyramid shaped frame was erected. Upon this was placed a large and varied collection of flowering plants. Canary birds, in cages, hung about the room and added the evening's entertainment by their tuneful warbling. The exercises consisted of singing and responses by the school, the instrumental accompaniment being played upon the organ and violin. Fiddle, canary birds and flowers at a Methodist service on Sunday night! What are we coming to, I wonder? Several members of the church refused to be present at the service because they disapproved of it, but the birds sang as sweetly, and the flowers bloomed as beautifully as if every member of the church had been there.

Sunday schools early made it a project to collect and send large numbers of eggs at Easter time to one of their denomination's orphanages. The Reading *Times and Dispatch* of April 16, 1870, reported:

A number of children connected with Trinity Lutheran Congregation sent off yesterday a barrel containing fifty-three dozen cooked and colored Easter eggs, as an Easter donation to the Lutheran Orphan's Home at Germantown.

A similar reference to this practice is to be found in the Pottsville *Miners' Journal* of April 18, 1876:

The St. John's Reformed Sunday School of Schuylkill Haven, as has been their annual custom for years, sent sixty-one dozen of eggs and twenty dollars in money as their Easter offering to the Orphan's Home, at Womelsdorf, Berks County.

Pennsylvania's Moravians, the nation's greatest early celebrators of Christmas and Easter, even distributed Easter eggs at their annual Easter service. The York *Daily* of March 29, 1875, wrote: "Every person who entered the church in the morning received an Easter egg on which was inscribed, 'The Lord is risen.'" The following year, according to the *Daily* of April 17, 1876, the order was reversed: The worshipers were presented their Easter egg token at the end of the service.

At the close of the service each one present was the recipient of an Easter egg on which was inscribed "All hail, the Lord is risen—Easter 1876."

MORAVIAN EASTER SERVICE

Though the Moravian Easter practice of waking their members with a "serenade" of trombones on Easter morning and marching in procession to their God's acre for an Easter sunrise service is not strictly in the province of this study, we shall nonetheless give our readers the best portrayal of this custom that has ever been written: an article from the pen of J. Max Hark, which appeared originally in the Lancaster *Intelligencer* of April 24, 1886.

The relentless spirit of modern "improvement" and "adaptation" has well-nigh obliterated from the cultus of that ancient church, the Unitas Fratrum, most of those peculiar and distinctive characteristics which once made its whole worship one grand living poem.

Only here and there, away from the track of ruthless progress, in some quiet country congregation, do we still occasionally meet with some of those quaint and original forms and customs that once were the everyday garb of the Brethren's church, and clothed her as with a halo of beauty and truth. Of all these, however, none can compare, for touching simplicity, and yet solemn and imposing grandeur, with the celebration of Easter morn in the little Moravian town of Nazareth, some ten miles north of Bethlehem, Pa. The same form of worship, indeed, is observed in Bethlehem, Lititz, and several other places; but in none can it reach the perfection of beauty that it here attains; for in none, as here, does nature lend her sympathy and aid, and help to make of all one glorious harmony.

The services during the whole Passion Week before tend peculiarly to devote and solemnize the hearts of the congregation. Every evening the worshipers assemble to read the pathetic story of the Saviour's life in the simple, unadorned language of the sacred Scriptures. Day by day, step by step, they follow him as he nears the final hour. On Maundy Thursday evening, in commemoration of the last meal with the twelve, they too gather with melting hearts, in Holy Communion round his table. On Good Friday at the hour when he is supposed to have given up the ghost, all engage in the beautiful liturgy used only on this occasion. It is a glorious requiem from first to last, sung and chanted in parts by pastor, by choir, by the whole congregation, and then again by the male and female portions separately, responsively comforting, exhorting, cheering each other; rising from a plaintive and mournful, dirge-like tone, to the joyous swelling sounds of a victorious hope and triumphant faith. Then all is silent and calmly peaceful again until the close of next day. A solemn stillness rests on the entire community. No business is transacted, no pleasure indulged in. It is the Great Sabbath. The Son of God is resting in the tomb; and around it in spirit all assemble as they come together in love-feast in the afternoon, preparatory to the great event of the following morning. With a mind thoroughly spiritualized and freed from earthly thoughts, the worshiper lays himself at rest, his soul hovering, as it were, between the sorrowful scenes of the past days, and the joyous anticipations with which believing hope awaits the morrow.

Very early on Sunday morning, long before the first penciling of dawn gives outline to the darkness, there mingle strangely with the sleepers' dreams the sounds of far-off soft and sweetest melody. Wafted from a distance through the fresh and fragrant morning air, like angels' whispers from on high they seem, so gently falling on the semi-conscious ear. Near and more near they approach. Slowly the dreamer awakes, and in rapture dwells on the mellow strains. It is the music of the trombone choir that thus early goes forth to usher in the gladsome Easter morn, and with its sweet old chorales gently arouses the slumbering villager, and bids him prepare for the worship of the day. The effect of this ancient custom on the mind surpasses all powers of description. It must be experienced, and then will never be forgotten. The profound stillness of the rural night, unbroken by the clatter of machinery, the roll of wheels, and restless tramp of feet, so absolute and perfect; the clearness and purity of the air at this most delicious period of the budding spring; the weird and touching sounds of the trombone, so peculiarly adapted to the music of the old chorals;

An engraving depicting a trombone choir playing at an annual Moravian Easter Sunday sunrise service.

together with the frame of mind induced by the services that have absorbed the attention of the entire previous week, and tended to make the whole soul more exalted and impressionable—all these help to make this part of the Moravian Easter ceremonies striking and beautiful beyond expression.

But it is only the introduction, the fit preparation for the service proper that is to follow.

Scarcely have the last strains of music died softly away ere the venerable old bell, strong and full toned, peals from the church steeple a warning loud and long, that now it is time for all to arise and repair to the house of the Lord. Simple toilets are soon made; the indispensable "coffee and sugar cake" hastily partaken of; and all assemble for the "Easter Morning Liturgy" promptly forty-five minutes before sunrise. The spa-

cious church is tastefully decorated with the floral offerings of the season artistically arranged, not by hired florists, but by the loving hands of some of the sisters, to whom the task is an act of true devotion and worship.

As the minister enters the chancel, the congregation reverently rises to its feet. Then with joyful voice he chants the glad announcement,

The Lord is Risen!

to which the full response is made by all, as if it were an echo from their souls,

The Lord is Risen!

And straightway from the lips of choir and people sung to the accompaniment of the full orchestra of stringed and wind instruments, ascends the grateful incense of gladsome praise;

ROUGHWOOD COLLECTION

An engraving of Moravian trombonists proclaiming the advent of Easter.

Hail, all hail, victorious Lord and Saviour,
Thou hast burst the bonds of death!

The rest of the Litany is a simple confession of faith, couched almost wholly in the chaste words of Scripture, interspersed now and then with some old hymn or touching chants, expressive of the deepest feelings of the heart. This ended, the service in the church is ended.

Then the worshipers, with the minister at their head, preceded by the trombone choir, form in orderly procession, and two by two take up their march to the cemetery, there to continue their devotions. Slowly they move on through the lone and quiet street, up the steep hill beyond the village, on the summit of which lies their beautiful "God's Acre," the tranquil, soothing stillness of the Sabbath morn unbroken, save by the trombonists' dirge-like strains.

According to a custom ever adhered to in the early settlements of the Brethren, the most elevated and choicest spot in the vicinity was always set apart for the hallowed repose of the dead. But in none of their communities in this country can there be found a graveyard that, for surpassing beauty in every respect, can compare with that which crowns the lofty hill just west of the ancient town of Nazareth. Almost in the center of a fertile plain, some twenty miles in diameter, it affords an unbroken view of not less than ten miles in every direction. North and westward the eye ranges along the mountain-bound horizon, resting now on the Delaware Water Gap, then on the Wind Gap, and, finally, on the Lehigh Gap. Southward it follows the course of the Lehigh River, along the base of the like-named range of mountains, until it flows into the broader Delaware, whose rising mists veil the Jersey hills, which bound the landscape on the east.

On every side, as far as eye can reach, a panorama rich and varied lures the gaze, from dark and shady woodland to bright and teeming farms; from green and velvety meadows to countless little hamlets and larger villages and towns.

Just at the foot of the hill nestles, calm and lovely, Nazareth itself, venerable and precious with its ancient buildings and historic associations. Along the eastern slope of the summit, in orderly array lie the graves of by-gone generations, the sexes scrupulously separated even in death, the departed brethren occupying all the space on one side of the middle path, and the sisters that on the other. Simple oblong slabs of marble, all alike in size and form, and lying flat upon the graves, speak to us eloquently of the truth, that death is the great leveler of distinctions; that rich and poor, high and low are terms only of that time that fleeth as a shadow, unknown in the mansions of eternity. On this morning, as on nearly every Sunday, loving hands have been busy adorning the green mounds with blooming fragrant tokens of remembrance until the whole space resembles one large garden, all aglow with fresh and brightest flowers of every form and hue.

Moving up the main pathway between dense walls of aromatic evergreens, whose branches interlock above and form a natural arched aisle, the procession at length halts and forms a wide semicircle on the highest point of the area. Above them the gentle zephyrs whisper softest music through the lofty pine and hemlock boughs. Before them stretches out the grand landscape bounded by the eastern hills. The early twilight purple, hazy veil rests softly over all the scene. The music is hushed. Then loud and clear the minister raises his voice in this declaration:

"I have a desire to part, and to be with Christ, which is far better; I shall never taste death; yea, I shall attain unto the resurrection of the dead: for the body which I shall put off, this grain of corruptibility, shall put on incorruption; my flesh shall rest in hope. . . . Keep us in everlasting fellowship with those of our brethren and sisters who since last Easter day, have entered into the joy of their Lord, and with the whole church triumphant, and let us rest together in thy presence from our labors. Amen."

Ah, what new meaning and real force these words attain thus uttered in the very presence, as it were, of all those dead! Standing in the midst of the graves of friends and kindred of more than a century back, how impressive, how comforting, how immutably certain the truth is felt to be, that the body

> is sown in corruption,
> *It is raised in incorruption:*
> It is sown in dishonor,
> *It is raised in glory:*
> It is sown in weakness,
> *It is raised in power:*
> It is sown a natural body
> *It is raised a spiritual body.*

Ay, doubt it who will, at that time and in that place, belief is a necessity. Each worshiper hears in his soul the combined testimony of all his honored ancestors and loved ones speaking from their graves. Their spirits bear solemn witness through his mouth. Life from the dead is a fact.

And now, as if in glorious illustration of the divine truth that is celebrated just at this point of the imposing service, there rises majestic over the dark horizon, up from his tomb of the night, the glowing lord of day. In gorgeous splendor he pours forth his golden beams. The fleecy clouds that seemed to hover like angels watching over his grave, now shining, glittering with refulgent glory, float upward on the radiant flood and disappear. In a moment the purple veil is lifted from the wide landscape, and all is bathed in brilliant light. Mountain top and fertile plain, forest, field and humble hamlet, all shine forth revived by the touch of the risen life. The night is vanquished; day reigns supreme. It is nature's Easter. The very trees above, around, are now made vocal with gladsome notes of praise arising from the tiny throats of whole flocks of little feathered warblers that found shelter in the dense green boughs through the long night, and now sing their songs of joy and welcome to the new-born day. At the same instant, as if transported to a higher sphere, and allowed a glimpse into the glories of the life and light beyond the skies, the trombones and choir astonished ask:

> *Who are these in bright array,*
> *This innumerable throng,*
> *Round the altar night and day*
> *Hymning one triumphant song?*

to which the congregation makes reply:

> *These through fiery trials trod,*
> *There from great affliction came;*
> *Now before the throne of God,*
> *Sealed with his almighty name,*
> *Clad in raiment pure and white,*
> *Victor-palms in every hand,*
> *Through their dear Redeemer's might.*
> *More than conquerors they stand.*

Like a victor's paean then strike upon the ear the closing words of the grand liturgy:

"Glory be to him who is the Resurrection and the Life; he was dead, and behold, he is alive forevermore; and he that believeth in him, though he were dead, yet shall he live.

"Glory be to him in the church which waiteth for him, and in that which is around him, from everlasting to everlasting. Amen."

The service is now ended, and all return to their homes, thoroughly prepared by this worthy introduction to the day the better to enjoy its remaining devotions. The semi-dramatic character of this quaintly beautiful form of worship brings the whole fact of the resurrection so vividly and realistically before the mind as to make an impression too profound ever to be forgotten. In the midst of all its soul-stirring associations and hallowed surroundings, the most hardened hearts must soften, the most careless be touched, and none can withstand the awe-inspiring, solemnizing influence of the occasion. There is something so peculiar in its strange mingling together of the real and the ideal, of sight and faith, of the material beauties of nature, and the spiritual truths of revelation, that it captivates the soul as naught else can. Faith, all glowing with delight, gently folds the spirit in her wings, and unresisting soars aloft with it to realms which ne'er before it had inhabited, but, where, exalted and entrenched, it fain would now make its abode forever.

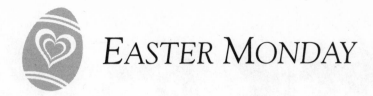

EASTER MONDAY

Up until recent decades Easter Monday was celebrated as a holiday in rural Pennsylvania Dutchland. Only the necessary farm and household chores were performed. The chief recreation indulged in on this day was to go visiting the *freindschaft*.

A former student of mine, Edwin P. Frankhauser, Jr., interviewed one Daniel Stauffer, of Lancaster County, a number of years ago for material for a term paper in his folklore course. Mr. Stauffer told my student:

Easter Monday is a day I shall never forget. When I was a young man I was out in the field plowing and everything went wrong. After a while I decided to go in and plow the garden, but in the garden I was almost killed by the horses who almost ran over me. Next I thought a while and I realized that this was Easter Monday. I called Mammy and said, "Get dinner and then we're going visiting." I never worked after that on Easter Monday.

Easter Monday was kept as a holiday from the earliest times on. The first reference in literature we have been able to find to our Pennsylvanians holding this day as a holiday is in a letter of Lt. Enos Reeves from Charlotte, North Carolina, dated April 8, 1782 (*Pennsylvania Magazine of History and Biography*, 1897, volume 21, page 468):

April 1, forded Deep River, and came into a settlement of Germans from Pennsylvania likewise; who were very busy in keeping Easter Monday, which is a noted time for frolicking among them.

At the turn of the eighteenth century Easter Monday was frequently set as a time for church dedications and shooting matches. In our early Pennsylvania history church dedications were great holidays.

The building committee would advertise the dedication in the newspapers, frequently announcing a two-day *Kirchweih*. Hucksters would appear in droves and set up their booths, selling refreshments to the throngs that came from far and near. Whiskey was ever present. When the force of the temperance movement began to make itself felt, the clergy began to rail against the hucksters, and finally drove them out. The Reverend William A. Helffrich, the noted Lehigh County Reformed clergyman, gives us an excellent picture of these conditions in his autobiography, *Lebensbild aus dem Pennsylvanisch-Deutschen Predigerstand* (Allentown, 1906).

Easter Monday was a popular time for parades in our county seats about the middle of the last century. The entertainment at these parades was frequently provided by groups of fantasticals.

Fantasticals, or fantastics as they were also sometimes called, were grotesquely clad men—young men usually, who paraded the streets on horseback, in wagons and sleighs or on foot in a noisy fashion on certain festival days, primarily on New Year's morning. The fantasticals were either the whole show—as on New Year's Day or First and Second Christmas; or they were incorporated as parts of a bigger parade—as on the Fourth of July, Battalion Day, Washington's birthday, or in Easter Monday parades.

The Allentown *Patriot* of April 12, 1849, described a parade of fantasticals on the previous Easter Monday:

The fantasticals. This peculiar and most wonderful company made its appearance in our streets on Monday afternoon. They

Fantasticals were a popular part of practically every parade held in the Pennsylvania Dutch Country in the nineteenth century. This scene is the illustration accompanying an article by Maurice F. Egan in Scribner's Monthly, *July 1881, page 350.*

made a strange and ludicrous appearance through their costumes, representing Indians, negroes, bustled women, etc.

A fuller description of a parade of fantasticals on Easter Monday in York in 1876 is given us in the York *Daily* (April 18, 1876):

Masquerade Parade. Our streets were greatly enlivened yesterday afternoon by the appearance of a masquerade parade, consisting of over 100 persons who appeared in as many styles of comic costumes. The parade was gotten up under the auspices of an organization composed of members of the Vigilant Fire Company, and known as the "Short-Haired Brotherhood" and another, composed of members of the Union Fire Company, and known as the "Blue Brotherhood." Each organization had with them a wooden steamer made so as to represent the real steamers, gotten up in good style and evidently cost considerable labor. They were good imitations of engines and the one drawn by the Short-Haired Brotherhood was so constructed that by means of a crank, machinery could be moved, representing the engine with balance wheel, piston rod and all. Places were fitted for fire, and smoke issued from a stack the same as a real engine. The Blue Brotherhood was accompanied by the Spring Garden Band, and the Short-Haired Brotherhood was headed by the National Cornet Band.

There were some ten or twelve vehicles in line and nearly the same number of mounted men were in line. One of the wagons contained a party representing negro minstrels. Another contained a crate in which was a man with several hounds.

The characters in line were comic, a number representing negroes. Quite a number represented females, some of whom were on wagons and several on horseback. Altogether the affair was generally admitted to be well gotten up, though considerable objection was made to the indecent conduct of several of the female characters and also the manner in which several of the male characters conducted themselves toward their female partners.

Military parades were popular in Philadelphia on Easter Mondays in the first half of the nineteenth century. We have a description of such a parade from the Philadelphia *Courier* of April 2, 1842:

The 28th net. being Easter Monday, and an annual parade day for many of our splendid volunteer corps, we observed those of the National Greys, Philadelphia Greys, National Guards, and some of the German companies. They looked as usual, *soldiers* from plume to spur, and handsome ones too.

The same newspaper of March 29, 1845, reported:

Easter Monday. Monday last was quite a holiday with multitudes of our citizens; and the farmers and operatives in the vicinity flocked to the city to see the fun and fashions. The National Greys paraded for the first time in their splendid new uniform of grey and gold, made after the exact pattern of the Boston Grays. The Philadelphia Greys, Captain Cadwalader, appeared for the first time in their new Regulation Blue Uniform. It is a picturesque and beautiful dress. The Union Greys, Captain Streeper, and Captain Baum's company of State Artillery also turned out in goodly numbers, and made a handsome appearance.

The urban festivities that were a part of Easter Monday's celebration began to decline in the post–Civil War days. By 1882 the Lancaster *Daily New Era* was saying: "The only public recognition of Easter Monday was the closing of public schools."

In fine, I shall quote an item from the April 14, 1879, issue of the Lancaster *Intelligencer:*

The secular observance of the Easter season is not nearly so general as formerly. Today—Easter Monday—there is no visible sign of the recurrence of the festival, other than the presence in the city of a large number of our rural friends in holiday attire, while during the day the streets have been alive with happy-faced boys and girls bearing in their hands baskets, a peep under the covers of which reveals the bright colored eggs that were yesterday deposited in tens of thousands of households the world over, by the ubiquitous rabbit in token of the joyous occasion, of which they have come to be regarded as strikingly emblematical.

THE EASTER RABBIT

The Easter rabbit is perhaps the greatest contribution the Pennsylvania Dutch have made to American life. It would be interesting some time to chronicle how this came about, how the Easter bunny conquered the nation. No doubt Easter commercialization, particularly the Easter greeting cards, produced in Germany, really won the battle, not to forget the millions of nineteenth-century German immigrants, who fortified the custom.

The Easter rabbit is entirely foreign to England, even to large parts of Europe. It was the Palatine immigrants of the eighteenth century who introduced him into our country and to our English-speaking neighbors. Wherever the Pennsylvania Dutchman migrated in the early decades of our history, whether south to Virginia, the Carolinas, or Tennessee, whether north into New York state or Canada—he took the custom of the *Oschter Haws* with him.

It must be remembered that the vast majority of the early English settlers in the Commonwealth—the Quakers and the Presbyterian Scotch-Irish—did not celebrate Easter. In fact, they even "shunned" it. The only exception were the British-Isles settlers of Episcopalian or Catholic background, but their numbers in the early decades of our history were extremely small.

Somewhere in the acculturational process the Easter rabbit came into the homes of Episcopalian, Quaker, and Scotch-Irish neighbors of the Dutch, very slowly, however, and in numbers small up to the post–Civil War period.[1] A writer in the West Chester *Village Record* observed as late as March 27, 1883:

The custom of supplying children with colored eggs on Easter day is a growing one here, although it has not been many years since it was almost an unknown feature of the Easter observance in West Chester. The custom is a German one, introduced into this country in its earliest history and ever since then has been steadily growing in favor among all classes in every part of the country until now it can almost be termed a National custom.

The Lancaster *Intelligencer* of April 10, 1882, still reported: "In the Presbyterian church there was an avoidance of any celebration of the Easter festival." It seems to have been the influence of the laity that changed the position of the anti-Easter denominations. Members of the nonritualistic churches even took the issue before the newspaper public. An irate Presbyterian, for instance, wrote to the Easton *Daily Argus* of April 10, 1882:

"Anti-Easter dogma" of the Presbyterian Church. Not even a word, or prayer, or any blessed and glorious resurrection hymns, were even alluded to in all of the services of yesterday morning. [The letter is signed,] Old Presbyterian.

It was not until the early decades of this century that the Easter party had won through on all fronts in Pennsylvania.

In the Pennsylvania Dutch Country the Easter rabbit always lays the eggs. The "rationalists" among us tell the children that the bunny "brings" them. Among our strictest religionists, especially among the Plain People, children are sometimes not told about the Easter bunny, just as they are not told about Santa Claus, "because," as they say, "this would be lieing." In families where the children are

This drawing of the Easter rabbit carrying a heavy basket of colored eggs was made for a little boy named Johannes Bolich of Brunswick Township, then in Berks County, now in Schuylkill County. Schuylkill was set off from Berks in 1811, so the drawing dates to 1810 or earlier. This may be the earliest portrayal of the Easter rabbit in America.

not taught to make nests for the Easter rabbit, the parents put gifts of Easter eggs and candy on the child's plate, where it is found by the children on Easter morning.

Childhood's greatest pleasure in the Dutch Country, next to the visit of the *Christ-Kindel* on Christmas Eve, has been—from the very first settlement at Germantown in the late 1680s on—to prepare a nest for the *Oschter Haws* (Easter rabbit). The children have always been taught that the *Oschter Haws* would come during the course of Easter Eve and lay—provided the child was well behaved—a nest full of beautifully colored Easter eggs.

Sometimes the children built their nests in the house (usually hiding the nest in a secluded spot, the egg-laying rabbit being somewhat on the shy side) or out in the yard, even sometimes, in the country, out in the barn.

Generally speaking the children set their headgear as a nest for the Easter rabbit, the boys their woolen caps or hats and the girls their bonnets. In some families the *Oschter Haws* was less timid and laid his nest of colored eggs on the child's plate set at the table. And the boldest of Easter rabbits merely deposited his eggs on the window sills—usually of great depth in the old farmhouses.

William J. Buck in a chapter on local customs in the 1884 *History of Montgomery County* (page 336) wrote:

The approach of Easter would be hailed with delight by the children, who would be induced to prepare snug nests, either in the house or some of the out buildings, for the coming of the *haas* or rabbit, and who would find therein next morning colored eggs said to have been deposited there by the aforesaid animal, who was widely known as the *Oster haas*.

In her book *Pennsylvania Dutch,* Phebe Earle Gibbons recorded several items of considerable importance in the Dutch Country. Her first observation (1882 edition, page 404) is that "in the three 'Dutch' counties of the east we have the rabbit myth more extensive than . . . in Lancaster." Regarding the nests she wrote:

A young man in Reading says that when they were children they always made a nest the evening before Easter Sunday, of an old hat or something similar, which they set near the door for the rabbit to lay the colored eggs in. . . .

At Easton a lady spoke of making nests for her two boys by taking plates, ornamenting them with cut paper in the form of a nest, putting into each a large candy egg and colored eggs, and placing a rabbit in one and a chicken in the other, and hiding them for the boys to find.

There is one important regional variant in the Dutch Country as far as preparing a nest for the Easter rabbit in the yard is concerned. In Lancaster County—the center of the Dutch Country's saffron belt—the *Oschter Haws* as often as not laid the eggs in the saffron bed. In Lehigh County where saffron was all but unknown the children, according to Mrs. Gibbons, before 1882 would take flax and make their nests under a bush in the garden. Professor H. M. Bowman, a native of Lancaster County, teaching in a midwestern university, wrote in the *Pennsylvania Dutchman* of June 9, 1949, about the importance of the saffron bed at Easter time in his youth:

Not only did the saffron bed furnish me the thrill of helping to harvest its crop in the last days of my summer vacation at grandfather's farm, but the next spring at our annual Easter visit it was again a source of pleasure. After the season of flowering in the fall this *Crocus* sends up a number of long dark green narrow leaves from the bulb, so that by late October the entire bed is a mass of long dark-green grass-like foliage. These leaves stay green all winter and then at Easter time Aunt Ellen

and our mother would hide a nest of colored eggs each for my brother and sister and myself in the saffron bed. It was an exciting thing to search through the tangle of thick green leaves and find one's nest of beautiful Easter eggs.

I have two more observations to make on the subject of the Easter rabbit's nest. In some families, I have been told, where a child misbehaved right before the time for the *Oschter Haws* to come the parents would tell the child the Easter rabbit wasn't going to reward it. The parents would fill the child's nest with rabbit pellets.

An elderly York County woman once told me that when their children were small they set their caps for the Easter rabbit also the day following Easter one season. She and her husband (they lived on a farm) went to the barn and got some *geils-gnoddla* (horse dung) from the stable and put it in the children's nests. They never after that, she said, set their hats for the Easter rabbit more than once a season. As at Christmas, some parents also put coals in the nest of disobedient children.

Sporadically I have found evidences in Pennsylvania of a special Easter cake in the shape of a rabbit shown laying a colored egg. The earliest allusion I have located to this practice in the commonwealth is in Phebe Earle Gibbons's article on Easter in her book *Pennsylvania Dutch* (1882 edition, page 404): "Literalness has gone so far in Allentown that I hear of cakes in a baker's window in the form of a rabbit laying eggs." Miss Frances Lichten described the cake rabbit in her volume *Folk Art of Rural Pennsylvania* (pages 231–232), as follows:

One of the really curious folk objects, representing another transplanted Germanic custom, was produced for the Easter celebrations by the local bakers. From the same dough with which they made their loaves, the bakers fashioned the Easter Rabbit which supposedly laid the eggs. On this bread sculpture they placed a raisin for the eye, and, in what is definitely a peasant-like conception, they inserted a dyed, hard-boiled egg in a position which furnished con-

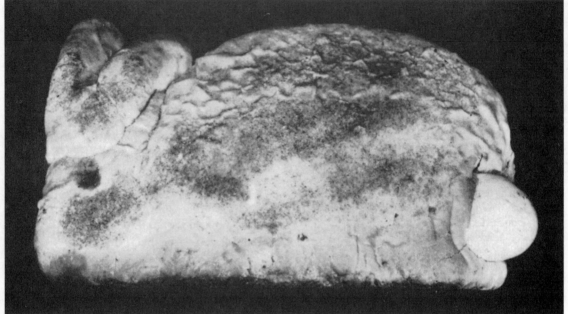

The Pennsylvania Dutch introduced the Easter rabbit into this country. Children were told that the rabbit laid the Easter eggs. Sporadically one comes upon cakes baked of bread dough in the shape of a rabbit, shown in the process of laying an Easter egg.

vincing proof to the child consumer that the rabbit was the source of the egg. The location for the egg was set by tradition. Though it was immodestly placed directly beneath the tail, the position was accepted unquestionably by all small children. But Anglo-Saxon delicacy winced when it noted the peasant directness of the placement, and the bakers, to mollify these American customers of theirs put the bright egg in the abdominal region. Even this was a little too strongly suggestive for the ultra-refined, who again registered their protests. Now certain chastened bakers, when they make the Easter rabbit for their clients, omit the egg, as a sacrifice to American prudery, leaving the rabbit with no visible evidence of his procreative ability to support the weight of the entire tradition.

In the fall of 1957 on a tour of Europe's folk museums, I visited the Volkskunde Museum in Basel, Switzerland. There was an exhibition of European Easter egg traditions. Included in the comprehensive exhibition were a number of cake or bread rabbits such as have just now been described. Upon my return to this country I put a query on my

weekly dialect radio program over a Reading station as to whether any of my listeners still baked a cake rabbit in the process of laying an Easter egg. I was put into contact with a Mrs. Russel Merwarth, of Easton RD, Northampton County, who has been baking such rabbits for many years for her family. And ever since, we have been presenting a cake rabbit to the many thousands of visitors at the annual Pennsylvania Dutch Folk Festival at Kutztown.

Rabbit games were popular in Reading at Easter parties some fifty years ago. There is a description of such a game in the Reading *Eagle* of April 9, 1911:

A "Bunny" game was indulged in. A large white sheet containing a picture of a rabbit with holes where the eyes should be was fastened over a doorway. One half of the little folks were then requested to go on one side of the sheet, while the other half remained on the other side. Those on the reverse side took turns looking through the eyes of the rabbit, and then a guess was made as to who was standing behind the rabbit.

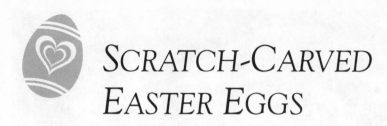

SCRATCH-CARVED EASTER EGGS

Pennsylvania's Easter eggs were occasionally ornately decorated. With a sharp knife or other pointed instrument one scratched through the dyed egg to the natural color of the egg shell. This type of decorating we call "scratch carving."

As a rule, the scratch-carved Easter eggs were presentation pieces. As such they were not eaten but cherished by the recipient and saved among other keepsakes. It is these scratch-carved Easter eggs, the early ones so expressive of our folk art, which have today become collector's items.

The earliest reference I have thus far located to the custom of scratch carving Easter eggs in the Dutch Country is in Thomas Anburey's *Travels through the Interior Parts of America* (London, 1789). The author speaks of boys and girls scratching all sorts of shapes and figures on Easter eggs with needles. However, we learn nothing about the designs themselves.

Judging from everything else that was ever decorated in the early period, we can be quite sure that there must have been tulips, flat hearts, and distelfinks. The very next reference, chronologically, does mention scratching tulips on Easter eggs. A Moravian, in a letter to the publisher of the Allentown *Republikaner* of April 23, 1829, writes that on a trip from Nazareth to Sumneytown he saw old folks scratching tulips on Easter eggs: "*Die alten kritzelten Tullpanen darauf.*"

What was scratch-carved on the early Easter eggs that survive other than tulips, the traditional motif in Pennsylvania Dutch folk art? The answer is: anything and everything from butterflies to elephants, besides, of course, the date and the recipient's name or initials.

The nineteenth-century newspaper press still directed itself primarily to the rural population. The columns were filled with periodic references to farmer so-and-so having brought into the newspaper office the largest rye or corn stalk, the heaviest pumpkin or the largest egg. Invariably the reference would end with: "Can you beat this?" And without fail this started others to bring in taller rye and corn, bigger pumpkins and eggs. Farmer vied with farmer, community with community. The "contests" were even carried into the out-of-county presses.

Scratch-carved egg decorated by a skilled fraktur artist.

A masterpiece in scratch-carved Easter eggs, illustrating the use of the traditional folk-art motifs of tulip and bird.

A goose egg, dated, and exquisitely scratch-carved in grandfather clock design.

One of the can-you-beat-this gimmicks in the decades from the 1860s and 1870s on was for the editor to mention, always shortly before Easter, that so-and-so had an early Easter egg, "probably the oldest in the county." There, of course, always was bound to be someone who happened to have an older egg. At least, this editorial trick has preserved for us a considerable body of information about early scratch-carved Easter eggs.

The editor of the West Chester *Village Record* of April 7, 1874, facetiously referred to this can-you-beat-it gimmick:

On Sunday we were presented with a handsomely colored Easter egg with our initials, and "1874" plainly and clearly cut thereon. We shall keep the egg in its soft cotton packing, and in future years, when another "the oldest Easter egg" fever breaks out, bring it forth and enter the lists for the prize in having "the oldest."

The Lancaster *Daily Express* of March 27, 1875, reported:

Many of our oldest inhabitants still have in their possession colored Easter-eggs presented them in childhood. During the past year the writer was shown some of these eggs that were "fixed up" away back in the last century, and, that had been handed down from one generation to another, until they had reached the third. Only a short time ago we were shown one of this sort by a gentleman living near Slackwater, this county. It was over one hundred years old, light as a feather, still retained its color and scratching, and was, as may be supposed, highly valued by the owner.

In 1884 the Lititz *Express* queried whether there was anyone in Lancaster County who owned an egg older than sixty-five years, the oldest one the paper had been able to unearth in Lititz. The Reverend Jacob N. Brubaker reported to the Mount Joy *Herald* of an old egg, formerly the property of one Mara Brubaker, which bore the inscription, "M. B. 1774."

There arose a whole school of professionals in the realm of scratch-carving Easter eggs, Abe Miller, of Lancaster, and Lyman Hess, of Lebanon, being the best publicized of them all. Among the lesser lights in the 1880s were C. A. Frailey and G. Washington Jack of Lancaster. Jack in 1880 scratched-carved an Easter egg for a niece, with the most unusual decoration that I have thus far heard about. The egg bore the young lady's name, the date March 28, 1880, a butterfly, with wings spread, and on the reverse side a monkey in soldier's clothes, playing a violin, while two goats are dancing to the music.

Scratch-carved Easter eggs were even brought back to Pennsylvania by people who toured Europe. The Lancaster *Daily Express* of April 11, 1871, carries an article about a Swiss Easter egg which one J. A. Sprenger, four years previously, brought back from his travels abroad. There is, by the way, a considerable amount of folk art today, in museums and private collections, dubbed as Pennsylvania Dutch,

Examples of delicately scratch-carved Easter eggs.

but pretty likely of the same origin as the Sprenger Easter egg.

There now follows a representative sampling of the type of newspaper articles our grandparents read in the Dutch Country on the subject of "the oldest Easter egg."

From the Chambersburg *Valley Spirit* of March 30, 1864.
We were shown, a few days since by Mr. L. F. Heck, several very ancient eggs. One was of a red color, beautifully ornamented by scraping, and dated on Easter day 1814; the other was dated 1825. These are certainly very old, but cannot be considered "good eggs."

From the Huntingdon *Globe* of April 15, 1873.
We were shown last week an Easter egg that is now sixty-four years old. It was first colored and the following inscription, together with some fancy work, scratched thereon: "Jane McNamara, Huntingdon, April 1809." The egg bears its age well; the shell is as hard as that of an ordinary egg, but the inside has dried up into a ball. The work on the shell was executed by Mr.

Brown hen's egg decorated with a gull-like bird; small animal; three turtles; decorative branch and leaves; bird on branch; small bird's nest with eggs; a fly or bee. Ends are highly geometricized. Inscribed "Edgar H Herr March 28 1869."

Isaac Dorland and it is now in the possession of his daughter, Mrs. Ann Massey, of this borough. We have heard of many Easter eggs that have been preserved by some of our citizens, but this one, we believe, is the oldest that has come under our observation.

From the West Chester *Daily Local News* of February 2, 1874.

Mrs. Wm. H. Price of West Chester has an Easter egg which was colored and given to a sick sister, (a child,) for amusement, in 1808 and since the decease of her sister, which occurred a short time afterwards, this egg has been carefully preserved because of its associations.

From the Reading *Times and Dispatch* of April 3, 1874.

Last evening we were shown by Mr. Lewis H. Neider, residing at No. 25 North Second Street, an Easter Egg of the year 1840. Inscribed on it is the year 1840, a log cabin, hard cider barrel, buckeye tree, the American flag, a sheaf of wheat, and mountain tulips. It is a veritable Old Line Whig egg, and was inscribed by the late Abraham Neider, the father of Mr. Neider, who prizes it as an old family relic.

Dark reddish purple hen's egg. The side area is divided into five equal parts containing a tree, a fish, a bird on a branch, the date 1877, and the inscription "Lizzie." The ends are five-pointed stars.

From the Carlisle *Herald* of April 9, 1874.

Who can beat it? Happening down town a few days since, we were shown a collection of Easter eggs, by our esteemed fellow townsman, Mr. Robert Noble, which for age, eclipses anything we have ever heard of. These were 1¹/₂ dozen in all, the oldest having been colored in 1821, the next in 1822, the two others in 1845. The dates of the others numbered down as low as 1858. We doubt if there is another collection of eggs extant, which can lay claim to the same date.

From the Carlisle *Herald* of April 1, 1875.

Every recurring Easter brings to light some Easter eggs, remarkable for age and beauty. John Shaeffer showed us one combining both these qualities. It was marked by Mr. S.'s grandfather, the late Fredk. Sanno, in 1813.

From the Allentown *Daily City Item* of March 28, 1878.

Dr. C. W. G. Schlemm, 240 Penn street, Reading, has an Easter egg that was colored, and beautifully scratched with a knife by his mother for him 52 years ago, in Maidencreek township, Berks county, when he was 4 years old. It was then of a dark brown color but has faded to a light brown, and is ornamented with the representation of plants in full bloom, one of which is in a flower pot. There are also floral wreaths around the ends.

From the Lancaster *Intelligencer* of March 18, 1880. Amos Miley, saddler, showed us this morning an old Easter egg which has a history. The egg was decorated fifty-five years ago by David Miley, Amos Miley's father, who was a wheelwright and then resided in Washington borough. On one side of the egg is drawn a mill with two large arches under it through which the tailrace water is supposed to pass. The mill is surmounted by a spire, the weathervane of which is a fish, very like a shad. The mill is flanked on either side by Lombardy poplars, trees that were held in high esteem in the olden time. To the rear of the mill, on the opposite side of the egg is a garden in which flowers are growing—one of them being a good representation of a tulip, and the leaves of another looking like tobacco leaves, a plant that was cultivated to some extent in Washington, even at that early day. On the centre of the larger end of the egg is scratched a double white star, and surrounding the star are the

Scratch-carved reddish hen's egg. Images include a tree; decorative branch and leaves; pig; nest with eggs; decorative tree; two turtles; small animal; house with large and small trees; cup with handle. The ends are geometric designs. Inscribed "E. H. H. 1874."

Brown hen's egg showing a box with two-branched decorative tree with bird on top; a long-necked bird; nest with eggs; ark; cup with handle; gull-like bird; small bird. Ends are highly developed geometric designs. Inscribed "1869."

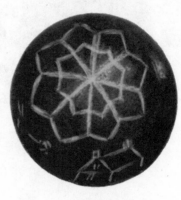

Brown hen's egg showing a house, decorative trees, initials "E A F," a bird on a branch, and highly geometricized ends.

following letters and figures: "D. M. B. S., 1825." "D. M." are the initials of David Miley, and 1825 is the year when the egg was scratched. The "B. S." is supposed to be the initials of some other person's name.

This egg was found about a dozen years ago in a secret drawer in an old-fashioned desk, and from that time until about two years ago was carefully preserved in his safe. Two years ago, Mr. Miley took it from the safe and put it in his coat pocket for the purpose of showing it to some friends. Forgetting that it was in his pocket he "sat down on it" crushing it into fragments. Gathering together the pieces, he placed them in the hands of Charles R. Frailey, esq., with a request that he should mend the egg if he could. Mr. Frailey took a large cork and cut it down to

the shape and size of the broken egg, as nearly as he could judge its proportions, and then piece by piece placed the fragments on the surface of the cork. There were 56 fragments and Mr. Frailey, with much labor and skill, succeeded in getting each one in its place, restoring the egg to its original appearance.

From the Reading *Eagle* of April 17, 1881.

Samuel Tea of this city has an Easter egg which was given to him in 1841 by his uncle, Henry M. Hain, who formerly lived in Pricetown, this County. On one side of the egg is a very good picture of an old-fashioned farmhouse, and on the other a drawing of a tulip with the figure "1841" in the leaves. The egg, the shell part, is in good condition without a crack.

Yellowish brown hen's egg depicting a large house with large and small trees; an ark; tulip and leaf. Inscribed "MAMA AND PAPAS GIFT TO THEIR BABY." One end reads "OUR BESSIE COLUMBIA APRIL 25 1886" in a circle.

Yellowish brown hen's egg has large and small vessels with sails spread; a bird; three rectangular designs; the initials "E A F"; the date "1883"; and "EASTER."

Yellowish brown hen's egg shows decorative flowers and leaves and a pair of flying birds. The end has "COLA" (is this for Columbia?). Most of the space is taken up by the inscription "BESSIES GIFT FROM MAMA APRIL 18, 1890."

Bright red hen's egg decorated with a heart and the name and date "LIZZIE CAMMAUF 1888." Otherwise plain.

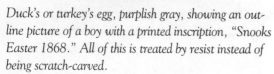

Duck's or turkey's egg, purplish gray, showing an outline picture of a boy with a printed inscription, "Snooks Easter 1868." All of this is treated by resist instead of being scratch-carved.

Dark brown turkey's egg shows a nest surrounded by two large fowl and six small ones; a palm-like tree; a box containing a decorative plant with a bird sitting on top. The ends are geometric in design. Inscribed "A.M.H. Marked by his Papa 1843."

From the Norristown *Register* of April 8, 1882.
Mrs. George Hallowell, of Lansdale, owns an Easter egg presented to her by her brother as a keepsake twenty years ago. It is beautifully marked with crossed American flags, with the date 1862.

From the West Chester *Daily Local News* of April 10, 1882.
Mary F. Torbert, mother-in-law of Major James E. McFarland, who is now about 78 years of age, has in her possession an egg which was boiled in 1816. It is an Easter egg.

From the Lancaster *Sunday News* of April 20, 1930.
[There follows a description of an early egg, engraved by one of the "monks" of the Ephrata Cloisters. This egg, which was in the collection of

the Lancaster County Historical Society, accidentally fell to the floor when being handled a number of years ago and disintegrated.]
The egg carried a beautifully etched reproduction of the crown of Great Britain. The intricate cornet is pictured on the token in all its complicated completeness. In addition to this central figure there are several other regal designs. For example the cornet is flanked by the thistle on one side and the scepter on the other side. It also carried the date "Easter 1776."

CONTEMPORARY DESCRIPTIONS
We have just presented the documentation for scratch-carved Easter eggs of old vintage. In the remaining pages of this chapter the reader will find

Hen's egg, brownish purple (lower left), ends spotted with lighter dots resembling a resist treatment. The inscription is scratch-carved "EMMA LOUISA 1855."

the contemporary descriptions of the newspaper press of the Dutch Country.

From the Lebanon *Advertiser* of March 31, 1875.
Mr. L. W. W. Hess showed us a number of Easter eggs, last week, which although executed with a pen knife, were very handsome. They had birds, flowers, &c., cut thereon, the artistic merit of which proves that Mr. Hess possesses the knack of engraving to a considerable extent.

From the Lancaster *Examiner and Express* of March 24, 1877.
Abe Miller, of this city, who is as expert in wood or other engraving as he is at wielding the bow—for who, in this community, has not been delighted with Miller's music?—has added another laurel by his exquisite carving of an egg, which he presented to Mr. Ringwalt, of East Orange street, who is a great chicken fancier. The engraving represents a bantam rooster and his brood of "chicks," and the work is certainly very fine.

From the Lancaster *Intelligencer* of March 30, 1877. Abe Miller, jr., is becoming quite noted as an engraver of Easter eggs. We were shown one today, on the shell of which he had engraved or "scratched" a very good likeness of a little girl. On the opposite side (if an egg can be said to have any sides, other than the inside and outside) was a representation of cupid astride a game cock. As an ornamenter of colored egg shells Abe can't be beat.

From the Lebanon *Daily Times* of April 3, 1877. Rev. J. F. Reinmund was the recipient of a handsome Easter present yesterday. It is a large goose egg colored dark brown, ornamental in the most elaborate style, evidently the work of an artistic hand. On the one end is a star, and on the other an anchor, the one pointing upward and the other, beneath a cross and crown imbedded in flowers, the symbol of steadfast hope. There is also a nest of eggs, a small bird on a twig, Holy Bible lying on mat, and the inscription: "To my pastor, Rev. J. Reinmund, from his catechumen, Calvin J. Houck."

From the Lebanon *Courier* of April 4, 1877. Mr. Lyman W. W. Hess, of this place, who is a first-class artist in putting up beautiful designs on Easter eggs, showed us one which he finished for Mr. Jacob M. Shindel, clerk in the Treasury Department at Washington. On one end of the egg is cut a star, on the other a rosette. On the surface is cut a wren, a full-blown rose with stem attached, the Goddess of Liberty and an Eagle bearing the inspiring word "Victory." Around the egg at one end is neatly cut, "by L. W. W. Hess, Lebanon Pa. March 27."

From the Lancaster *Intelligencer* of March 20, 1880. We were today shown by Abe Miller, four colored eggs which have been scratched by him, and which will be shipped to Brooklyn, a party from that city having ordered them some time ago. One of the eggs has a correct likeness of Horace Greeley on one side, while on the other is a coat-of-arms of Pennsylvania. On a large goose egg Mr. Miller has scratched pictures of Wilhelm, the violinist, and Miss Ann Teresa Berger, the cornetist. Another goose egg contains an excellent picture of Henry Ward Beecher on one side, while on the other is a picture representing a tobacco packer and his boss. On the fourth egg is scratched a picture of the Berger family of musicians as they appear on the stage. The

Small, brown hen's egg with two decorative trees; a circular geometric design; the initials "S A K"; and the date "1846." One end has a large crawling turtle.

work is remarkably well done, and it shows that Mr. Miller is quite an artist in that line.

From the Lancaster *Intelligencer* of March 27, 1880. Abe Miller, the decorative artist of Easter eggs, has pictured a nest of them for Mr. R. J. McGrann's children, which are among the choicest specimens of his skill yet produced. One of them for John McGrann depicts a boy taking piano lessons from Prof. Matz; Miss Eleanor McGrann's has a representation of a girl reading a newspaper, another with a girl washing a piece of china is for Miss Harriet G. McGrann; Richard J. McGrann, jr., has a picture of the horse "Betty," Hugh McGrann's a pony and Grace McGrann's a baby. Each has engraved upon it the name of the child for whom it is intended and the year of his or her birth.

From the Lancaster *Intelligencer* of April 10, 1880. The Reading *Times and Dispatch* has a notice of an egg which was sent to Mathias Snyder of that city by a friend named Shields of Lancaster. It has a fire engine scratched on it with the name of the Rainbow fire company, No. 1, of which Mr. Snyder is a member. The work was done by Abe Miller of this city.

Reddish brown hen's egg decorated with a weeping willow; pick; shovel; axe; farm wagon; plow; and the date "1870." The ends are plain.

From the Lancaster *Daily New Era* of March 28, 1882.

Abe Miller, musician and artist, is again engaged at this old work, engraving Easter eggs. His latest efforts are in the matter of engraving a portrait of the lamented Garfield, on one egg, and a portrait of Washington, the "Father of His Country," on the other, with a representation of a small boy, a rabbit and a miniature egg on the reverse. Both are in the usual artistic style for which Mr. Miller is noted, and they were made to the order of Dr. H. H. Gerhart, of Canandaigua, New York.

From the Lebanon *Daily Times* of March 24, 1883.

Mr. Lyman Hess, barber, of this place, last week forwarded to Gov. Pattison an Easter egg which is artistically engraved with representations of the Goddess of Liberty, the American eagle with a streamer in its mouth, with the words "Democratic victory"; a rooster, crowing the words, "40,000 for Pattison"; and a rose, encircled by stars. The egg was very much admired by Gov. Pattison and he has returned his thanks to Mr. Hess for it.

From Lancaster *Daily New Era* of April 1, 1893.

Wm. Sultzbach, day clerk at the City Hotel, is the happy possessor of a beautiful Easter egg, which was presented to him this morning. It is artistically decorated with the figure of a very fat man blowing a horn and a spirited equine representation, illustrating one of the contestants in a Roman chariot race. The decorative work was performed by Abram Miller, who is the greatest artist in that line in Lancaster city and it is one of the best specimens of his skill.

From Lancaster *Daily New Era* of April 4, 1896. [Description of Abram Miller's engravings.]

One egg has etched on its purple-colored surface a dog riding a dog, a Zebra and a bunch of Easter lilies. Another contains a crowing rooster, a peacock, with spreading tail, a setting hen and a rising sun. Another is decorated with a plump cherub juggling with an Easter egg almost as big as the cherub itself and containing the inscription "Easter, 1896."

From the Reading *Eagle* of April 14, 1911.

Decorates eggs with pictures. One of the most novel ideas for preparing chicken eggs for Easter is that of drawing pictures of rabbits, squirrels, roosters, and other small animals and fowls on dyed eggs. The method was adopted by John H. Howard, who resides at 415 Laurel Street, Reading, Pa., several years ago. He was formerly a cobbler, but for the past five years was unable to work owing to ill health. Every Easter he has adorned several hundred eggs for which he finds a ready sale. After the eggs are dyed, Mr. Howard takes a cobbler's repairing knife and outlines the pictures. The eggs are attractively decorated with fowl heads, bunnies, chipmunks, storks, and other designs.

THE EASTER EGG TREE

One of the most remarkable things that happened in the past decade has been the nationwide acceptance, almost overnight, of the custom of decorating a tree with colored eggs at Easter—all brought about by the appearance in 1950 of *The Egg Tree*, a children's book by Katherine Milhous, a Philadelphia author.

Is the Easter egg tree an old Pennsylvania Dutch custom? To answer this question is the purpose of this chapter.

My conviction as of this moment—based on documentation which I am about to present—is that (1) putting up an Easter egg tree in one's home was an innovation in the second half of the nineteenth century, a novelty yes, but very definitely not a custom; and (2) impaling blown eggs—most frequently undyed ones—on a bush in the yard at Easter time is of much older vintage and must be considered a custom of the Pennsylvania Dutch Country, though certainly not a widely practiced one.

First of all, I shall present the evidence I have been able to collect on the subject of putting up an Easter egg tree in one's home. There are three documents from the nineteenth century.

From the Reading *Eagle* of April 24, 1876.
Easter Egg Tree. R. D. Lingle, druggist, at Tenth and Chestnut, has in his parlor, for the pleasure of his little daughters, a new kind of tree, which was placed there on Easter Eve, and has been called an "Easter Egg Tree." It is probably the only one of its kind put up in this city, and is apparently a new idea. Spruce boughs are hung with egg shells beautifully ornamented with paint, gilt, and colored paper. Beside these are paper ornaments

representing bouquets, goddess of liberty, "Cross anchor and heart" combined, hanging baskets, banners, flags, etc., all tastefully arranged. Excepting the eggs, the tree presents very much the appearance of a Christmas tree.

From the Lebanon *Daily Times* of April 3, 1877.
An Easter Novelty. On Sunday last we were shown an Easter decoration that was quite a novelty. At Christmas time evergreen trees laden with choice and rare gifts, etc., are very common, but a similar tree adorned with mottled and vary-colored eggs is an unusual adornment for the house, to please the children and excite their fancy. It made a beautiful appearance and was quite as appropriate as the time-honored Christmas tree.

From the Norristown *Register* of April 11, 1887.
An Easter-Tree. Ex-Councilman Harry C. Smith celebrated Easter yesterday at his home, No. 505 Astor street, by having a large cedar tree placed in his parlor, standing in the middle of a miniature garden. The tree was tastefully festooned with easter eggs, all handsomely decorated, and presented a very pleasant and attractive scene. Rabbits and little ones were pleased, as well also the crowds of little folks who thronged his residence yesterday afternoon.

SOURCE OF THE IDEA
Naturally, we do not know the source of the inspiration for putting up these three trees. The idea may possibly have come from seeing an Easter card picturing the egg tree (such cards, produced in Germany for the American market, were widely disseminated), or the idea may conceivably have been inspired by written accounts. An instance in point is the following illustrated article on the Easter tree from *Lothrop's Annual* (1895):

The Easter-tree is a delightful feature of the Easter season in Germany. It is not so universal as the Christmas-tree; for in Germany there is no household so poor but the Christmas-tree finds a place in it, even though its branches may spread scarcely wider than the flowers of a good-sized bouquet. The Easter-tree is more common in northeastern Germany than elsewhere, and the tree-frolic is something all young people ought to know about.

For an Easter party, at which the frolic is to take place, a large tree, set upon a good-sized table, stands in the center of the room. The larger the room the better. The tree is hung with *Oster Eier* (Easter eggs) of every color and size. During the year the children gather many varieties of birds' eggs and save them for decorating the Easter-tree. Hens, geese and turkeys' eggs are also colored by boiling them in solution of dye-stuffs—a strong one to make the deep colors, a weak one for the more delicate shades.

Loops of bright-colored ribbons, always of contrasting shades, are pasted upon the eggs to hang them by, tip downwards. Tinsel ornaments and pendants; curious sugar people; cake animals, especially lambs and rabbits; Easter hens, and chickens; and dainty chocolate and sugar confections of every conceivable variety are fastened to the boughs, while underneath, upon the table or pedestal, sitting in special state, the wonderful Easter rabbit, or sometimes the Easter lamb, presides over the gifts and favors concealed in the *Oster Hase's* nest.

In other words, knowledge about an Easter egg tree became commonplace in the Dutch Country—as elsewhere in the nation—about 1900. Two items I am about to quote will bear this out. In the April 1908 issue of the *Pennsylvania German Magazine* (page 182), Mrs. H. H. Funk, who edited the Home Department, wrote in connection with Easter:

In some parts of Germany the Easter tree repeating the Christmas tree is in favor but the Pennsylvania Germans have not accepted it but have instead the Easter egg and "Oster Haas" which have been handed down to the present time. The Easter trees in Germany were decorated with eggs of every bright hue that were blown clear then filled with dainties, sometimes gilded and suspended by narrow ribbons.

ROUGHWOOD COLLECTION

Indoor Easter egg tree illustrated in Lothrop's Annual, *1895.*

A member of the staff of the Reading *Eagle* of March 23, 1913, wrote (his source obviously Mrs. Funk's article):

In some parts of Germany, the Easter tree, repeating the Christmas tree, is in favor, but in Pennsylvania, Germans have not accepted it; but, have instead, the Easter-egg and "Oster-Haas," which have been handed down to the present time.

This about covers the subject up to the year 1936. What happened since then as far as the Easter egg tree is concerned would fill a volume alone. In 1936 appeared the most influential book

Easter egg tree and Easter putz of 1947, the creation of the late Mrs. Elmer Palsgrove.

ever published about the Dutch Country—Cornelius Weygandt's *The Blue Hills*. In this book Weygandt wrote an intriguing chapter, entitled "Easter Eggs and Egg Trees" and he included a photograph of an Easter egg tree erected by Mrs. E. Palsgrove in her Reading home.

When I became curator of the Berks County Historical Society in Reading I invited Mrs. Palsgrove to show her Easter egg tree with its thousand and more colored eggs at the society. She accepted. In due time Kathleen Milhous came to see the Palsgrove tree and the children's book *The Egg Tree* was conceived, which since 1950, as I have said, has single-handedly made putting up an egg tree almost a national Easter custom.

I shall not write more about the indoor Easter egg tree, only to say that I have had to revise through the years, as more information came my way, my early view and statements on the egg tree as a Pennsylvania Dutch custom.

EGGS ON BUSHES OUT IN THE YARD

At the outset I made the statement that impaling eggs, most frequently undyed ones, on a bush in the yard at Easter time is an old, though not a frequently practiced, custom of the Pennsylvania Dutch Country. German and Swiss folklore publications, which remain quiet as to the custom of putting up Easter egg trees, make frequent mention of the use of eggs on bushes, particularly such as are carried about in Spring festival parades, not on Easter Sunday to be sure, but in the weeks immediately preceding.

I have been able to find informants in all sections of the Pennsylvania Dutch Country who have knowledge of decorating a bush with undyed eggs at Easter time. Below I shall now present my evidence for saying that this was an old-time Pennsylvania Dutch custom.

On April 30, 1957, Sarah Ritzman, eighty-nine, of Tower City told me that when she was twelve

KATHERINE MILHOUS COLLECTION

Easter egg tree greeting card, European in origin, of early 1900s.

years old she was a maid in the John Coleman family of near Gratz, Dauphin County. At Easter, she said, the family impaled brown eggs, natural color, on a bush in the yard. Mrs. Walter Evans of Sunbury told me a number of years ago that her mother and grandmother put up egg trees before her. The Harold Hack family, of Mexico, near Mifflintown, have put up decorated bushes in the yard for long years. Mrs. Hack's mother, who died some eight years ago in her seventies, used to tell how her

The late Mrs. Elmer Palsgrove's Easter egg tree exhibited in 1949 at the Berks County Historical Society. The tree is strung with electric lights.

MARION B. WILSON

Thorn bush Easter egg tree.

Guild of Pennsylvania Craftsmen Easter egg tree.

Easter egg tree by Olive Newcomer.

mother put eggs out on a bush in the yard when she was a little girl on a farm in Mifflin County.

William Edgar Artman, supervising principal of the Warriors Mark-Franklin Joint Consolidated School, wrote me in 1948:

Prior to 1929 the Clyde Artman family (of which I am a member) lived on Mann Avenue in Yeagertown, Pa., at which place and for a number of years we had an Easter egg bush. For weeks prior to Easter we ate eggs which we had blown out of their shells to color for the bush. The bush was a large pink rose bush which I believe is still standing at the same spot.

TITUS GEESEY AND KATHERINE MILHOUS

An outdoor Easter egg tree at Shartlesville from the year 1950.

Since 1945 Mrs. Grace Sprankle of Alexandria, Huntingdon County, has been displaying an Easter egg tree on the front lawn of her home. Several thousand egg shells are used to decorate the tree.

The Gable sisters, Mollie and Emma, of Waldeck, Lebanon County, told me on March 25, 1953, that their mother at Waldeck used to impale blown eggs on a bush out in the yard at Easter. Mrs. Milton Kintzer, then of Myerstown, Lebanon County, told me in 1953 that she put up an egg tree out in the

yard for the children when they were small—in the 1920s and 1930s. According to Mrs. Kintzer, a Mrs. Carson Spittler who used to live in Myerstown put one up considerably before that time.

An elderly couple, Mr. and Mrs. John McQuate, of Denver RD, Lancaster County, have been placing natural colored eggshells on the branches of a bush out in their yard each year during the Easter season for long years. Mr. McQuate reports the custom was handed down from his mother's family.

ROUGHWOOD COLLECTION

Outdoor Easter egg trees at Topton Lutheran Home.

Leonard E. Shupp of Fullerton tells me of a Mrs. William D. Wright, of Mechanicsville, Lehigh County, who up to a few years ago put up an egg tree in the yard for long years. A Mrs. Emma Thompson puts one up in the yard in Walnutport and did so prior to that time when the family lived in Palmerton and Pennsburg.

In fine, I must repeat that this is a custom met with *only* sporadically, like, in fact, most folk beliefs which are only found here and there and not, like the custom of the Christmas tree, found in well-nigh every home in the Gay Dutch Country, the Plain Dutch—Amish, Mennonites, and others—to this day to a man refusing to put up a Christmas tree.

ASCENSION DAY

In Pennsylvania Dutch folk religion, Good Friday and Ascension Day are the holiest days of the Christian year.

Somber days they were, both of them, truly holy days and not holidays. How different, utterly different, from the other church festivals in Dutch Pennsylvania, each one characterized by a festive mood all its own.

Work, in house, barn or field, was strictly forbidden on these days. The rural folk firmly believed that lightning would strike the person or property of any woman who sewed on Ascension Day or any farmer who as much as drove a single nail on this day.

The no-sewing-on-Ascension-Day theme and its meaning to our folk, past and present, comes beautifully to the fore in two items from the folklore archive of the Pennsylvania Folklife Society. One is in a letter, dated December 16, 1948, from an eighty-one-year-old woman living in Baltimore. She wrote:

I was born and partly raised in Manor Township, that is in Lancaster County and that surely was a Dutch section. I could not speak a word other than Dutch until I went to school and then it went very hard with me. Did you ever hear about Ascension Day, that no women would sew or do any ironing on that day for fear that at some time the lightning might strike them? In my younger days I done dressmaking and I always got strict orders from the women who had dresses at my place at that time that I was to be sure not to work at them on that day.

The second item illustrating the work taboo is from a 1950 folklore term paper of one of my students at Franklin and Marshall College. A fraternity man, he wrote:

This past Thursday which was Ascension Day I approached our cook and asked her if she would please sew a tear in one of my dress shirts. It was the only clean one I had left and I needed it for that night. She has always done little favors like that for the boys ever since she has been here. She gave me a sorrowful smile and said, "I would do it for you, Bob, on any other day of the year but this." I couldn't for the life of me figure it out, so I had to ask for an explanation. "It is Ascension Day, and if you do any sewing with a needle, lightning will strike this house." Knowing the temperament of our cook, I let it go at that.

From among hundreds of folktales I have collected on the subject of someone who worked, particularly sewed, on Ascension Day and the consequences, here are a representative half dozen or so.

Told by Minnie Steffy, seventy-six, of near Red Run, Lancaster County, on February 23, 1953:

One time there was a funeral on Ascension Day and during the funeral service a horrible thunderstorm arose. The minister stopped preaching and said to the people if there was anyone in church who wore an item of clothing sewed on that day, that that person was to get up, leave the church and quickly take it off. A woman got up and went out. She was wearing an apron which she had finished just that morning. She took it off and hung it outside on a fence and came back in. After the funeral service was over and after the storm had passed, when she came for her apron, lightning had burned it to ashes.

Told by Mrs. Cora Snyder, about seventy, of Jefferson, York County, on February 25, 1953:

There was a woman who wore a bonnet on Ascension Day which she had finished on that morning. A thunderstorm came up. She became frightened and took off the bonnet and put it on a fence post. A moment later a stroke of lightning hit the bonnet.

Holy-Day Stories:

CHRISTMAS,   GOOD FRIDAY,

EASTER,

ASCENSION,   WHITSUNTIDE.

——o——

TRANSLATED BY
R. H. SCHIVELY.

——o——

PHILADELPHIA:
Reformed Church Publication Board,
54 NORTH SIXTH STREET.

The title page of a Reformed Sunday school story book on church festival days.

Told by Mrs. Harry Senft, about fifty, of Jefferson, York County, on February 25, 1953:

One Ascension Day a hired hand on a neighbor's farm put a cluck with the chicks out in a coop. It needed a little repairing, so he went for a hammer. The farmer saw him and told him: *"Schlag narriyeds ken naggel hie uff Himmelferdawg."* (Never drive a nail on Ascension Day.)

Told by Mrs. Thomas Shaffer, about seventy, of Meiserville, Snyder County, on February 27, 1953:

My mother, Mrs. Frank Phillips, who used to live at Palace, told me that when she was a young woman she bought a new hat on Ascension Day at Kantz. On the way home lightning struck to the right of her and to the left of her. My mother used to tell that she threw the hat down in the road. She wouldn't take it home.

Told by Mrs. Harvey Hughes, about fifty, of Roedersville, Schuylkill County, on May 8, 1957:

My grandmother used to tell of a woman who got ready to do some sewing on Ascension Day. As she took the scissors in her hand to cut a piece of cloth *"iss ra die schare ausnanner gfalla."* (The scissors[1] fell apart.)

Told by Mrs. Benjamin Bachman, about seventy-five, of Palmerton, Carbon County, on February 28, 1959:

They used to tell of a stone mason who was setting up a stone wall one Ascension Day and a thunderstorm arose. A bolt of lightning struck the wall and blew it all to bits.

Quakeress Phebe Earle Gibbons, the author of the book *Pennsylvania Dutch,* incidentally the most important volume on the folk culture of nineteenth-century Pennsylvania Dutchland, cited a similar instance (1882 edition, page 398):

A simple-minded woman in Lancaster County, who showed some regard for the Reformed Church, said that she had sat up late sewing the night before, so as not to sew on Ascension Day. "My mother," she said, "knew a girl that sewed on Ascension day; and there came a gust and killed her."

The Reverend F. K. Levan, in an article "Maxatawny Prior to 1800" (*Proceedings of the Pennsylvania German Society,* 1894, volume 4, page 85), posed the question that many a reader probably has in mind at this very moment:

On Ascension day no woman would use a needle, nor allow one to be used. The point of this we never could see. Had it been on Good Friday we would have assumed a connection between the thought of the needle and the spear which pierced the Saviour's side.

The reason for the thunder lore in connection with Ascension Day is to be found in the fact that it always falls on Thursday, which in dialect is *Dunnersch-dawg.* And *dunner* in Pennsylvania Dutch means thunder.[2] This is an important instance of word magic in our Pennsylvania folklore.

Among the work taboos there is one against sweeping the house on Ascension Day. Phebe Earle Gibbons, in her volume cited above (page 398), wrote:

You will find many strange ideas, such as that on a certain church festival, say Ascension day, you must not sweep your house, lest it becomes full of fleas.

Among a list of superstitions in Dr. Preston A. Barba's *"Eck"* in the Allentown *Morning Call* is this one, similar to the one just given: "If you sweep on Ascension Day ants will get into the house."

The most interesting lore I have collected about Ascension Day concerns sweepings. An eighty-nine-year-old woman, Sarah Ritzman, of Tower City, told me in 1957 that when she served as a farm maid in the Gratz area in her girlhood, they customarily took the sweepings and placed them in a bag and carried them on Ascension Day morning to the nearest creek that flowed *"gaiya oovet"* (towards the west). It was believed if the sweepings were thrown in the creek *"kaimd ken ungetsiffer ins haus"* (no vermin would infest the house). A daughter, present at the time I interviewed Mrs. Ritzman, said the family continued this practice in Tower City in her own youth.

In our folklore archive there is a letter from Miss Ida Hollenbach, of Saegersville, dated February 20, 1953. It concerns lore she collected from a Mrs. Amelia Hildenbrand, then seventy-eight years of age, of Mount Carmel. Miss Hollenbach wrote:

On the day before Ascension Day it was Mrs. Hildenbrand's mother's custom to sweep the house and from each room take a bit of the dirt and collect it in a container. Next she went to the barn, the hen-house, and pig sty and picked up more dirt to add to the other. Even from the yard itself she gathered up a handful of soil. Then on Ascension Day she took the whole to the boundary line between their farm and a neighbor's and threw it over the fence. This was meant to keep the home place free of insects and bugs during the year.

Ascension Day was the most popular day in the year for fishing in the Pennsylvania Dutch Country.

One recreation was universally practiced on this day in Dutch Pennsylvania: One went fishing. In fact, one now and then encounters the nickname "Fishing Day" for it. Matthias Zahm's diary for 1836 makes note of this sport (*Lancaster County Historical Society Proceedings*, volume 47, 1943, page 66): "Thursday, May 12th Assention day, Henry Moyer, Aaron Traeger & Godfried Zahm went fishing this morning, with rod & line."

The reason for going fishing on Ascension Day is to be found in the sympathetic magic formula of *similia similibus*: like creates or generates like. Jesus ascended into Heaven on this day; so likewise on this day fish will rise up out of the water. It is as simple as this!

One of our early collectors of Pennsylvania Dutch folklore, Dr. Walter J. Hoffman, in an article in the *Journal of American Folklore* (1888, page 131), cites another recreational aspect to Ascension Day:

One will frequently observe, even at this day, the bodies of birds of prey, with outstretched wings, nailed against the gable ends of barns. Birds of this kind, shot upon the farm, were thus exposed to keep away others. A quarter of a century ago it was the custom for the young men to organize a party and shoot all obnoxious birds, and frequently those beneficial to the farmer, on Ascension Day.

An Ascension Day activity participated in by all areas of Dutch Pennsylvania was going out into field and forest to gather wild herbs, teas, and special kinds of flowers. Teas made from plants gathered on this day were believed by the folk to possess an unusual health-giving power.

The number of herbs or teas to be gathered was considered the all-important factor by the folk, seven and nine being the numbers most frequently encountered. By drinking seven kinds of tea on Ascension Day one would escape contagious diseases for the rest of the year, it was believed. A tea made from nine species of herbs was used to cure a

fever. C. M. Bomberger, in an article "Almanacs and Herbs" in the May 15, 1950, issue of the *Pennsylvania Dutchman*, tells us a maid on his parents' farm in the Lititz area of Lancaster County kept the family always well stocked in all kinds of herbs and teas. He wrote:

On Ascension Day Lizzie gathered nine plants for medicinal purposes, three from the woods: dogwood flowers, elder blossoms, winter green; three from the field: cinquefoil, catnip, ground ivy; three from the garden: horehound, sage, thyme.

We encounter the principle of *similia similibus* in connection with teas gathered on Ascension Day. Thomas R. Brendle and Claude W. Unger, in their volume *Folk Medicine of the Pennsylvania Germans* (1935, page 170), wrote: "All herbs to be used for diarrhoea or dysentery are to be gathered on Ascension Day, a day not good for things descending."

A former student of mine, after a visit with his classmate's parents in Strausstown, Berks County, reported his friend's recollections:

There is a certain little white flower, the name of which he could not remember, which they as children used to pick only on that [Ascension] day. They would put them in a bag and put it away some place in the house and leave it there for an entire year. This would protect the house from being struck by lightning for the entire year. The procedure had to be renewed every Ascension Day.

I have one more folk remedy to report concerning Ascension Day. It is one I collected from Agnes Wendt of the *Grubba Karrich* section of Snyder County in 1951. She said if one cuts his corns on Good Friday and then again on Ascension Day they will disappear.

George F. Moore, a Dunkard farmer from near Lawn, Lebanon County, and one of the best folklore collectors we have in the Dutch Country, submitted this bit of weather lore to the Folklife Society folklore archive: If it rains on Ascension

Day, rain will be of no help all summer long, because there will follow a dry wind each time. In Dauphin County, according to an article by E. L. Knohr (*Pennsylvania Dutchman*, May 15, 1951, page 6), there is a folk belief that if it rains on Ascension Day all the acorns will be drowned. Dr. Edwin M. Fogel, in his *Beliefs and Superstitions of the Pennsylvania Germans* (page 262), lists this item: Water from Ascension day rain will cure sore eyes.

In the eighteenth century, the Reverend F. K. Levan tells us (*Proceedings of the Pennsylvania German Society*, volume 4, page 85), the boys and girls were confirmed in families of Lutheran and Reformed persuasion on Ascension Day. "Girls," he wrote, "were confirmed in white dresses, and they wore white caps."

Early Pennsylvanians of British-Isles background—Quakers and Scotch-Irish—in their opposition to the Pennsylvania Dutch celebration of church festivals dubbed these practices as "Dutch Popism." The church holidays struck these fellow Pennsylvanians as most strange. Christopher Marshall, the Philadelphia diarist, sojourning in Lancaster, entered in his diary under date of May 4, 1780: "great holiday with the Dutch, called Ascension Day."

WHITSUNTIDE

Whitsuntide is a term more British than American in usage. It designates Whitsunday, the day in the Christian calendar that commemorates the descent of the Holy Spirit upon the Apostles, and Whitmonday, celebrated as a secular holiday.

Unlike the other days of the year we have been treating in this study, Whitsuntide is characterized by a striking paucity of folk beliefs. In fact, there is in the Dutch Country but one widely held superstition—a bit of weather lore—regarding Whitsunday: If it rains on Whitsunday there will be rain on the following seven[1] Sundays. The only other regional folk belief pertaining to this day is one recorded in Edwin M. Fogel's *Beliefs and Superstitions of the Pennsylvania Germans* (page 239): "Rain on Whitsunday means no chestnuts."

In the Pennsylvania Dutch Country up until a generation or two ago Whitsunday (*Pingshta* in dialect) was the time for confirmation among the Gay Dutch, Lutherans, and Reformed. The Reverend Thomas R. Brendle, the eminent collector of our folklore, wrote in this connection (*The Pennsylvania Dutchman*, November 15, 1951, page 7):

Confirmation was a time for new clothes for the children to be confirmed. The girl got two dresses,[2] in some sections a colored one for confirmation and a white one for the first communion. The young boys usually wore their first pair of long trousers at their confirmation. It was a general custom for parents to forbid their children to engage in courtship before confirmation.[3] Whitsunday became the day for the change from the dark clothes of winter into the white garments of spring. At present it has been supplanted by Easter.

Two instances of food specialties in connection with Whitsunday have come to my attention. Historian William J. Buck, writing in an article entitled "Customs" in the Doylestown *Bucks County Intelligencer* of August 16, 1859, said:

The German settlers observed customs from their fatherland, such as masquerading on Christmas; the *spruch*, and shooting on New Year; the rabbit at Easter; the doughnuts on Shrovetide; and the wheaten loaf at Pinxter.

Rather intensive questioning on the part of the author of older people in Bucks County through the past ten years has not brought any information to light as to what Buck meant by a Whitsunday "wheaten loaf."

The other bit of food lore in conjunction with Whitsunday I collected in the Pennsylvania Dutch settlement at Markham in Ontario, Canada. A Mrs. Simeon Reeser told me that the old folks always used to serve egg cheese[4] (called *tsiear-kase* in dialect) on this day.

Dialect *Pingshta* has added one choice item to our folk speech. In Lancaster and Lebanon counties, when a woman's slip shows, one says to her: "*Du husht Pingshta fer Oshdra.*" (You are celebrating Whitsunday before Easter.)

In Pennsylvania Dutch the word for lilacs is *Pingsht-blumma* (Whitsunday flowers, literally). Though lilacs were found in every farmyard, I have never collected any folk use of this bush, excepting that in more recent times (after cemeteries began to be divided into family lots and before cemetery associations came into existence) it was the custom of the farm women on Whitmonday of each

The square in early Lancaster, the site of the annual Whitmonday celebrations.

year to clear the family graves of weeds and briars and then to decorate the lot with lilacs.

I first learned of Joe Pinkster Day (also pronounced "pingshta") from Elizabeth Clarke Kieffer, the former reference librarian of the Franklin and Marshall College library. Miss Kieffer has this name for Whitsunday from her mother, who spent her youth in Lancaster city. On Joe Pinkster Day, according to Miss Kieffer's mother, the young, unmarried girls would wander the streets of Lancaster, counting blue neckties. (All the boys, it seems, made it a practice to wear blue on *Pingshta*.) The girls believed that the wearer of the twenty-first blue necktie they counted on Joe Pinkster Day would become their future husband.

A reporter on the Lancaster *New Era* staff, in describing the decline of Whitmonday as a holiday in Lancaster, wrote (May 26, 1890): "As a day of pleasure in Lancaster, 'Joe Pfingsta' is a past number."

Up until a generation or two ago Whitmonday was considered one of the main holidays of the year in the Pennsylvania Dutch Country. Almost 175 years ago, on Whitmonday, May 15, 1780, to be exact, Christopher Marshall, who was sojourning in Lancaster at the time, entered in his now famous diary:

I went nowhere from home this day although it's a very high holiday in this place, and as it was a most pleasant, agreeable, fine day, numbers were diverting themselves abroad, some riding, some walking, others playing long bullets, &c.

Today only the Amish, the "horse-and-buggy" Mennonites, and a mere handful of our older Gay Dutch any longer celebrate Whitmonday as a holiday.

How did our early Pennsylvania Dutch folk spend Whitmonday? By taking in Battalion Day at Hamburg, say; or by coming to town—to York, Lancaster, Reading, or Easton to see the sights.

There follows a most readable account of a Whitmonday, a battalion day, in Hamburg, Berks County, from the Reading *Gazette* of May 22, 1869:

The annual frolic came off Monday. Early in the morning the prospects for rain were about as good as "croakers" would have them in time of drought, yet the people flocked hither from the city and from Pottsville in large numbers. Every little town and township of Berks County was represented by the sturdy son of the farmer with his handsome carriage and his fiery steed, *un alle de schaene maid* [and all the pretty girls] from near and far were present. Though all these people were disappointed at not seeing the soldiers, "Fader Abraham," and the flying circus, everything had the appearance of battalion day, and all seemed to feel repaid for their visit.

Dancing at the hotels was kept up from eight o'clock in the morning until late last night, and some in their joy jumped themselves almost breathless. We saw a woman come out of the room with perspiration rolling down her face, her waterfall hanging down on her back, and throughout she had the appearance of a woman that was about to be taken to the lunatic asylum. She sank down in a corner, and after a little rest was again sailing on the "light fantastic toe" to the delight of the spectators, who would encourage her by saying, *"gay nigh Sal,"* and she did go in—into hysterics an hour afterwards.

Being disgusted with this scene, we visited the second floor, and here we found three men perched upon a store box going through the motions as though they were sawing wood, and indeed the "fiddling music" sounded just like it.

This place was "ram" jammed full of human beings, and it was impossible for us to reach the spot where the dance took place, and we had to make observations from a distance, and looking over the crowd we could see the heads of the dancers pop up and down, which reminded us of Old Lindsay's show days, when Mrs. Woffelbach and Jacob Schunelheimer performed behind the canvas to the response of Old Lindsay. At this time we heard some one say that he had lost his pocket book, and though we did not have much money with us, we began to feel alarmed and left. On the sidewalks were tables and store boxes loaded with oranges, *zuckerstengel,* lemonade, ice

Musterings of the local militia, known as the Badalya *(from the word "battalion"), were often held on Whit-Monday and other Dutch holidays. They featured token drilling and elaborate parades, at the tail end of which were usually bands of "fantasticals." This parade appears to have even an elephant involved. The cut is from H. L. Fischer's pioneering dialect book,* 'S Alt Marik-Haus Mittes In D'r Schtadt, Un Die Alte' Zeite: En Centennial Poem in Pennsylfanisch Deutsch *(York, 1879). The title can be translated: "The Old Market-House in the Center of Town, and The Times of Long Ago: A Centennial Poem in Pennsylvania Dutch."*

cream, ground-nuts, peanuts, and *grundniss*. The girls and boys, the men and women, would promenade up and down Main Street, with an orange in one hand and a mintstick in the other, and in many instances they would come forward in line, holding each other by the little finger, and encircle a bashful lad who would be standing on the pavement, with the entreaties,

"Cum Jeck, du muscht treata." In order that "Jack" would not be considered a miser, he like a man, walked up to the stand and purchased a mintstick for each one.

Thus the streets were kept alive, some were standing on the curbstones gnawing away at an orange and chatting, others in the middle of the sidewalks were pushed about from one place to another, while men would lean against the buildings and gaze with wonder at the population.

At about 2 o'clock a "horn" was heard sound up town, when the hue and cry went forth that the Band *spiehled,* and there was a general stampede for Popp's Hall, from which place the band started out. They paraded through the *principal* streets followed by about 10,000 children—more or less.

BATTALION DAYS UNCOMMON AMONG PLAIN DUTCH

In areas where the Plain Dutch predominated, battalion day Whitmondays were less popular. Instead, the rural folk spent the holiday by coming to town. The reason that the county seats—the market towns—were so well frequented on Whitmonday is that this holiday became the substitute for the two-day June fairs which, having fallen into ill repute, were voted out of existence by borough councils around the 1830s.

In the period from about 1835 to the time of the Civil War and even some years later, Whitmonday in Lancaster was the greatest gala day of the year. It was called the "Dutch Fourth of July." Great crowds of people from all the rural districts streamed into the city; long excursion trains brought thousands more from as far away as Reading and York. The York *Democrat* of June 7, 1870, wrote: "Quite a number of our young folks visited Lancaster, where Whit-Monday is kept as a universal gala day." The Columbia *Spy* of May 26, 1866, reported: "The faithful turned out on Monday to celebrate their dear *Pfingsten.* It took an extra train to carry this motley crowd into Lancaster."

The schools were closed on Whitmonday. The industries shut down. Only the stores remained open. The York *Daily* of May 26, 1874, reported:

The large shops were nearly all closed, and very few mechanics were at work. The public schools were closed. Though the stores were open, not much business was done.

The great crowds came to Lancaster on Whitmonday to eat and drink and to be amused. What tickled the palates of the "country cousins" in the 1860s, say? Primarily peanuts and *lebkucha* (gingerbread), ice cream and candy.

Peanuts, frequently called groundnuts in an earlier day (hence the dialect term *grundniss*), in the 1870s sold at five cents a pint. Vendors could be heard from one end of the market square to the other, yelling at the top of their voices: "Peanuts, *Grundniss*; Lemonade, *Tsucker-wasser.*"

The most difficult thing for me to understand is the universal popularity of *lebkucha,* the cake on which Dutchmen feasted at funerals, fairs, and vendues. *Lebkucha* were particularly popular among the Amish. A correspondent of the *Bucks County Intelligencer* of January 9, 1878, who signed himself "E. M.," gives us an excellent description of the Amish in Lancaster County. In alluding to their great liking for this cake, he wrote that in Ohio their English-speaking neighbors called *lebkucha* "Amish Feed." The Lancaster *Intelligencer* of June 2, 1879, in a write-up of Whitmonday activities, reported that *lebkucha* went at "an average of five cents per square foot." What appetites our great-grandfathers must have had!

Peanuts and ice cream vied for tops in popularity on Whitmondays in the long ago. They were even selling "hoko poky" (hokeypokey) in York as a Whitmonday specialty back in 1886. The *Columbian* of May 26, 1847, in its Whitmonday coverage, carried the headline: "I Scream! Ice Cream!" Who would have thought that the childhood rhyme "I scream for ice cream" was this old!

My favorite Whitmonday "ice cream" story is from the Lancaster *Intelligencer* of June 7, 1870. Two young couples entered one of Lancaster's prominent ice-cream saloons. They were attired in regular country costumes. The boys were tanned brown by exposure to the sun, while the faces of the girls were ruddy as apples. Seating themselves, they called for "two five-cent saucers of ice cream and four spoons." On being informed that ten cents a saucer was the lowest price at which the luxury was sold, the innocent and happy quartette said they would take "one saucer of cream with four spoons!"

On a Whitmonday in the long ago it was no uncommon sight to see a couple of country girls walk up to an unaccompanied young man and ask for a treat. And the lad, by custom, was bound to unloose his purse string and buy them some candy, *moashey* perhaps, or what is more likely, mint-sticks—*tsucker-shtengel*.

Newspaper accounts of Whitmonday tastes reveal that other foods besides peanuts, *lebkucha*,

candy, and ice cream were also reveled in: bananas, oranges, and popcorn, all in 1877.

To quench a Whitmonday thirst, the most popular drink was lemonade, which came in a score of shades. "Lemonade from the palest yellow to the ruddiest red was sacrificed at the astonishingly low price of 'two schooners' for five cents," reports the Lancaster *Intelligencer* of June 2, 1879. Eight years earlier the lemonade is described as only "tinted." It just goes to prove that even great-grandmother liked her pop in the rainbow colors of today.

Other drinks were ginger beer (1866), soda water (1867), and "scotchineal" (1871), whatever that may have been. But there was more than just small beer: There was lager beer and whiskey, too,

Early American Militia Company, from a drawing by George L. Brown, 1835.

and plenty of it. One of the Lancaster papers in 1883 suggested the name Whitsuntide should perhaps be changed to "Whiskytide." Strong voices were raised against even continuing Whitmonday as a holiday as a result of these excesses.

Whisky ruled the day. If this be Whitsuntide, for heaven's sake let it die; and if it can't die a natural death, let the people and the press take hold of it and *choke* it

wrote the Lancaster *Daily Express* of May 21, 1872. It was widespread drunkenness, incidentally, which earlier had brought the spring and fall fairs into disrepute and consequent discontinuance.

A much more restrained voice—and a more tolerant and realistic one, too—was lifted in York when it came to condemning the excesses of this holiday. A member of the staff of the York *Dispatch* wrote in the issue of May 12, 1883:

In a moral sense, our manner of keeping Whitsuntide is rather a profanation than otherwise, for the festival was appointed by the church, to commemorate the descent of the Holy Ghost upon the apostles. The whole week preceding it, was devoted to prayer and supplication, and it was, in the whole, considered sacred by the primitive fathers. Be that as it may, however; young America will enjoy itself on Whitsuntide Monday, and it would be foolish and unprofitable to attempt to put it under restraint. Youth has its season of rejoicing, and old age will come soon enough without putting a pair of spectacles upon both soul and body, before their time.

People came to town on Whitmonday not only to eat and drink; they wanted to be amused, too. So around Center Square one found the booths of the itinerant vendors of patent medicines, showmen with snakes and fat women, persuasive individuals with everything from "Shoe Blackening" to "Razor Powder." But alas, about the time of the Civil War the city fathers refused to license these vendors any longer, and with their passing from the scene Whitmonday in Lancaster lost much of its drawing power. A reporter on the Lancaster *Intelligencer* of May 17, 1869, wrote a eulogy on the medicine man:

The crowd in town is not so large as usual, and the absence of the Medicine Man, Blackening Man, Soap Man, and Showman from Centre Square leaves a void in the day's proceedings that is not filled. The eloquent and persuasive tones of their voices are not heard, their manly forms are not present—it is the play of Hamlet with the part of Hamlet left out.

It has been with us heretofore a pleasing duty to listen to these itinerant orators: long have they amused us. True we made no purchases; but others did, and as the stamp dropped into the willing hand of the orator, the tones of his voice grew still more musical and resonant, and his praises of his stock in trade still more assured and wonderful.

We entered the tented shows, what snakes, what dogs, what owls, were presented to our gaze. How our eyes feasted upon the strange phenomenon of hairless dogs and tail-less cats.

But now the practical city fathers have ordered things differently. "Those days are gone and beauty is *not* here"—not by a long sight. No, this Whit-Monday wasn't a success.

OTHER WHITMONDAY AMUSEMENTS

There were horse races, rope walkers, bands, balloon ascensions, velocipede races, trained mice and monkeys, stereoscopic views, and dancing. Even implement dealers set up exhibits on the Square in Lancaster as early as 1866 to show the newest in farm machinery: "Self-Rakers attached to a reaper."

Then there were the flying horses.

Large numbers of persons visited these revolving horses, most of them, however, simply to see them in operation. All such stopped only a moment to look on, or "passed by on the other side." A great many "went in," and took a seat on a "horse" or in a "coach," paying five cents each for the privilege, and were whirled round at a rapid rate for a few minutes

reported the Lancaster *Daily Express* of June 11, 1867.

A balloon ascension, a common Whitmonday feature in Lancaster, around 1868.

Hotel and museum in early Lancaster, two focal points for Whitmonday crowds.

In the early 1880s the Italian balloon men began to appear on the scene. And there were toy vendors, too, of course. One of the most entertaining of these curb salesmen in 1876 was a glib-tongued fellow who sold a toy by which he was able to make successful imitations of a mockingbird, a poodle dog, a pig, and other animals. He gathered quite a little audience wherever he went, selling his whistles for ten cents, or:

> Three for a quarter,
> One for yourself, your wife, and daughter.

He mounted a stand near the depot in the afternoon and was handling a brisk trade when the mayor wandered up, and sensing that the boy was selling without a license, let him know it would be better to leave. The boy did so, muttering that "one hundred years ago we fought for our liberties; now we are denied free speech!"

During the Civil War the young blood from the country frequently had their pictures taken on their annual Whitmonday visit to Lancaster. Photograph and ambrotype galleries did a rushing business. Incidentally, it is of interest to note what a reporter in the Lancaster *Daily Evening Inquirer* of May 25, 1863, had to say about the effect of having so many of the young men away in military service. He wrote:

Before this unnatural war that now desolates the country, broke out, a "turn out" was generally made up of one good looking girl and a bashful young man seated in a fine looking buggy, whirled along at a rapid pace by a spanking horse; now the "turn out" consists of *two* good looking girls, and a young man anything else but bashful, thus proving that us lords of creation are increasing in the estimation of the fair sex.

The stores were open for the most part on Whitmonday to catch the trade of the "country cousins," especially that of the gentler sex, who seized this opportunity to buy their spring attire. Someone noted in 1875: "On this day a class of people make purchases who do not buy at any other times, and who perhaps never see the city except on this day."

After the Civil War, Whitmonday crowds began to diminish. The York *Dispatch* of May 14, 1883, commented:

The old custom of making it a holiday for pleasure or frivolity has gradually been dying out. Even in Lancaster, where Whit Monday was formerly the biggest day of the year, and the sidewalks crowded with people, the crowds have been perceptibly diminishing during the past few years. As the people grow in intelligence they give up their old notions and customs and take a more rational and reasonable view of these things, and besides, our American people are getting so much in the habit of making money, that business and money making will at any time take the place of recreation and amusement. Few of our holidays are now spent as they were in the good old days of "the long ago times."

The Lancaster *New Era* of May 25, 1885, wrote:

A good many will come anyhow, whether there is anything to be seen or not. The young folks of opposite sexes from the rural

districts meet on this favored day and enjoy themselves as best they may, and it is at least a relaxation from work. The day is not what it once was, but it is still honored because it is venerable, rather than for any special joy or pleasure that it brings.

A writer in the Reading *News* of May 15, 1880, put his finger on a not unimportant reason why Whitmonday was so long the most popular community holiday in Dutch Pennsylvania:

In many respects Whit-Monday has a great advantage over other holidays. Coming as it does, in probably the most pleasant season of the year, when nature is in one of her most agreeable moods; when the flush of beauty and the charm of an inspiring temperature is upon the face of all things. It is really the first prominent holiday that can be counted upon or made use of safely for an indulgence in out-door sports and pastimes; the winter having passed, and in its company the wet and chilly weather, which so uniformly characterizes the early spring. In this latitude, the time and the hour is seized upon for a frolic.

As I have already indicated, one of the reasons that Whitmonday lost its popularity was that the city fathers, by prohibiting patent medicine vendors and other mountebanks from selling their nostrums on Center Square, robbed the holiday of its big circus and country fair character—the very factors that drew the crowds. And with the passing of the razor powder man (in 1855 he even appeared "in the full costume of the last century"), the soap man, and the tooth powder man, also died the glory of Lancaster's "Dutch Fourth of July."

We shall now present a representative number of the best contemporary accounts of Whitmonday in Lancaster.

From the Lancaster *Hive* of May 23, 1804.

Last Monday, being *Whitsuntide,* was religiously, piously and sanctimoniously observed, and hallowed, with all the Christian decency usual on those occasions. Apprentices, servants, kitchenwallopers and pot-wrestlers, in the sanctity of their hearts, too pious to labor on this holy day, in large congregations commem-

The square in early Easton, scene of markets, fairs, and Whitsun frolics.

orated the occasion in the devout exercises of fishing, gunning, caballing, horse-racing, ball-playing, dancing, drinking, swearing—not working. Would pious Christians work on a holiday?—No master shall ever compel such devout souls to violate a holy holiday by working: no, in spite of all masters, and of all mistresses too, they rested from labor, for it were a sin, a first rate sin, to work on Whitsuntide.

The mechanics too [pious souls!] religiously observed this holy day, and rested from their labor. Like the primitive saints they assembled themselves together, they communed with one another in brotherly love, and where two or three were met together, there the glass was in the midst of them, to bless them—that is, to make them happy; for many of them were as happy as Chloe.

The militia too, in their zeal, celebrated the day with all due military éclat: and black eyes and bloody noses at the same time gave proof of the piety and bravery of the soldiery.

The piety of the merchants was announced by shut shops: that is, the windows. True, the doors were open, and if needy customers had money, it were hard to turn them away: but the windows were uniformly closed—locked fast—and if any business were transacted, the windows being shut, Omniscience did not know it—knew nothing about it.

And a great deal of business was done that day, a great deal of money was taken, for the country people were generally in town—and, though the windows were shut, it was a good day for the store-keepers.

This farce was kept up all day long, but God Almighty knows nothing of the matter: a great deal of goods were sold, but he does not know that—not he—for the windows were shut, and one may do what one pleases, if one keeps one's windows shut:—nor shall he ever know it; for we will keep our windows shut, and we are not going to inform upon one another. *Sacro Sanctus.*

From the Lancaster *Intelligencer* of June 6, 1843. Last Thursday, if it had been twenty years ago, would have been Fair Day; but, to no one's surprise, the streets were duller than usual. Even memory, as we regarded the quiet afternoon, could hardly realize the scenes that occurred here abouts even ten years ago, when the merry laugh, and the jocund swain with his blooming partner, made the streets resound with joy! Yesterday, Whit Monday, saw the town swarming with visitors from the country; but they seemed to be of another character from those who made up the populace on the Fair Days. Such is the force of Improvement. It has already as sensibly affected old customs, as it has ancient errors. We regret that the customs cannot still be innocently observed.

From the Reading *Gazette* of June 15, 1867. Years and years ago, long before the writer of this article was born, the annual Fair Day in June was the great day of the year in Lancaster, just as it was in Reading. When it was abolished, Whit Monday was substituted in the former city, and ever since it has been the day of days there.

In the days of Hugh Lindsay ("Old Hans"), he was the great centre of attraction on this day. We recollect him well as he was wont to ride through the streets attired as a clown, and the hundreds of little urchins, and very frequently men and women, too, who followed him to listen to his funny sayings at the different street corners, where he would stop to hold forth in his peculiar way. "Old Hans" is gone, but his place has been taken by others, who, although not as well versed in the art of tickling the feelings and exciting the risibilities of their listeners, yet manage to extract a goodly number of "stamps" from the pockets of the people who come to town to see the sights.

From the Lancaster *Intelligencer* of June 2, 1868. Whit-Monday is a great day in Lancaster. From time immemorial it has been set apart as a holiday, and the country folks have religiously devoted it to fun and frolic. The corn is planted, and harvest has not begun. This is a pause at this period in agricultural labor, and the brawny lads and buxom lasses from all parts of the country came to town to see the sights!

Early in the morning the long line of buggies, with fine fat horses, which have taken the place of the Conestoga teams, and garlanded hay-ladders of the past, begin to stream into the city. The change is one rather for the better, and shows the advance of civilization in our midst. As we look at the fresh complexioned, full-breasted and round limbed Lizzys or Betsys, we are tempted to envy Hans or Jake, who rides and drives in complacent self-importance beside them. From every direction they come until our streets are full of masculine brawn and female beauty.

The city folks have not been forgetful of the coming flood, and every possible device is resorted to for the purpose of inducing our somewhat green country cousins to leave their greenbacks behind them. Boogy Hambright has a show in one corner of Centre Square, and such a show, four boys blacked with burnt cork, and as ignorant of music as so many pigs, constitute what is paraded as "a full band of Ethiopian Serenaders." Two naked dogs, such as may be seen running through the street any day, and a couple of stuffed owls constitute a menagerie, to depict the wonders of which taxes all the intellect of the proprietor, as he stands outside and bawls himself hoarse with his even more exaggeration than those invented by him during the shad season.

On the opposite corner a serpentine cuss who looked like a cross between an itinerant scissor's grinder and an excommunicated Yankee preacher had pitched a tent, within which was kept up all day long a beating of barbarous drums, which would have put to shame Japanese festival music or the banging of a dozen Chinese war gongs. People held their fingers in their ears as they passed along the streets, and the Mayor was repeatedly petitioned to abolish the nuisance. It was a day of license, however, and both Boogy and the crape hatted and solemn visaged humbug, with one snake and a pale looking boy who swallowed a small sword semi-occasionally, were permitted to take our country cousins in as often as they pleased.

Right in the centre of the Square stood a covered wagon with the unmistakable odor of decaying fish about it, while a nondescript reprobate continuously called out to the gaping crowd, "Here's where you gets a sight of the great sea whale, *for only ten cents.*" Paying their money for themselves and their gals, our rustic friends got sight of a common sturgeon, which we have no doubt many of them took to be a genuine specimen of the identical fish which made a meal of Jonah.

The well-known Matthew Gebler and the Mulatto Indian held forth in another corner in opposition to each other, Matt selling blacking with remunerative rapidity, and the Zambo disposing of some sort of a medical humbug with equal facility. Both seemed to be raking in the dimes.

All along the streets were stands where pink colored lemonade was disposed of to the thirsty crowd, while the rush upon the ice cream and lager beer saloons was tremendous. Gingerbread was the staple diet, and the cracking of ground-nuts a universal epicurean recreation. Photographs were in demand, and many a country beau paid for a dozen counterfeit presentments of his lassie. The flying horses and carriages were still an object of attraction, but alas! they had degenerated, so far as motive power is concerned. A gang of boys, who take it time about in riding and turning by turns, has taken the place of the sturdy steed which once stepped so proudly while whirling his fair freight in rapid revolutions. This is an evidence of the dying out of the old time sports which deeply touched the sympathetic nature of a prominent bachelor councilman, and we could not help sympathizing with him in his lamentations over the decaying glories of this great Lancaster County holiday. Still the lads and lasses patronized the Five Points institution, and we saw more than one country maiden exhibit a pair of suggestively neat ankles as they whirled around on the well cushioned wooden horses.

As the day wore on many of the boys began to exhibit symptoms of fatigue, and it was evident that not a few of them had piled up loads of lager beer larger than they could conveniently carry. Through the streets the crowd surged in happy good humor, however, and all passed off pleasantly. By 6 o'clock the town was almost deserted, and the boys and girls had gone home to talk the affairs of the day over in old fashioned country courting matches, protracted it may be until the chickens crowed to announce the coming of the dawn. That is part of the performance, the delights of which will never grow old, while human nature remains what it is. With each returning June it will be renewed, while buds blow and blossoms unfold the glad sunshine, whether Whit-Monday continue to be a holiday, or be merged into the crowd of common days, of which no note is taken.

From the Lancaster *Intelligencer* of June 7, 1870. Whit-Monday. This ancient holiday which has been observed time out of mind by the lads and lasses of the rural districts of our county, is gradually but surely going into a decline. The flying horses that erst delighted the young of both sexes as they swung around the circle with wonderful rapidity, having already been numbered among the things of the past, as have also the booths formerly erected for the sale of small-beer, tough pies, peanuts, and instead of fond lovers walking arm and arm along the streets with little fingers hooked, and lips sweetened with "horsey-cakes," the demoralized young country men are now-a-days apt to betake themselves to the beer saloons and indulge in lager and bagatelle, while the young women feast their eyes on the fascinating millinery and other gewgaws of fashion that adorn our shop windows. While the mothers were happy in their girlhood in purchasing and performing on their favorite instrument, the accordion, of which one firm used to sell hundreds every Whit-Monday, many of their daughters aspire to the more fashionable and costly melodeon and piano.

The decline of Whit-Monday observances was particularly noticeable yesterday. Although the day was fine the streets were not nearly so thronged as heretofore, nor did the crowd present its usual rural and rustic appearance. Many of the beaux and belles could scarcely be distinguished in dress and style from our less robust but more roughed city ladies. There were a few noticeable exceptions however.

Very few of them visited the races at the Park. The charge of 50 cents admission, and 25 cents additional for a ticket to the grandstand, being regarded as an exorbitant extortion.

From the Lancaster *Daily Express* of May 20, 1872. Whit-Monday dawned bright and beautiful; yet, with all the auspicious circumstances of good weather and good times, the day was far behind its usual glory in the matter of a large crowd and "lots of fun." There was really nothing to be seen—no provision at all made for the reception of our country cousins, if we except the cake and lemonade stands, with their dust-covered confections and ice-cold drinks. Barnum has come and gone. The "Big Injuns" have had their day, and their council fires are extinguished. What then, could have been expected today? Very little, we assume—and those who expected *little* were certainly not disappointed. The Whitsuntide of former days is gone—irretrievably lost; we fear it can never be resurrected. Well may we exclaim, with Byron—"Those days are gone, but beauty still is here." We have a beautiful city, and a great many beauties of the fair sex graced her streets today; but the grand old Lancaster County carnival day was but the shadow of its former self. The problem is easily solved, the schoolmaster is abroad. The common schools have done their work, and the taste for big crowds, flying carriages, puppet shows, and negro minstrel performances has (happily) been removed. A picnic by our German friends of the Swiss Gruetli Society, a country dance at Gerz's cottage, an organ grinder here and there, and a set of flying carriages near the Locomotive Works, made up the total of today's amusements. Alas, poor Whit-Monday! "Gone, but not forgotten!"

From the Lancaster *Daily Examiner* of May 25, 1874.
Thousands of anxious eyes watched the dawn of today. For weeks the plans and arrangements of our country cousins have all been directed with but one object—the visit on Pingshta. This day is emphatically a Lancaster day, and is as peculiar to our country as the Carnival to Rome, or Mardi-Gras to New Orleans. Other neighboring counties observe today, but the festivities common to Lancaster are widely discussed all over the state as a peculiarly Lancaster institution.

For days and weeks busy hands have been preparing the finery with which to deck the fresh beauty of the rural lassie. The coachmaker has had imperative orders to have the first new buggy of the young man coming of age finished, without fail, by Whit-Monday. The shining set of new harness was long ago carefully hung on the garret, with fervent hopes of a bright morning, so that the four-year-old may look his best when the youth drives over to the neighboring farm for the two blushing girls who weeks before, at meeting, promised to go along to town.

But the day has lost much of its rollicking spirit that was characteristic of fifteen or twenty years ago. The young folks no longer crowd upon the flying-horse, as in days of old, and the sight of the couple from the interior lovingly seated in a flying-carriage is becoming more rare. We will see here and there the bashful swain and shy maiden, bearing the evidences of rustic surroundings, walking with brown fingers interlaced, viewing the wealth of candy stores. But Pingshta still has many of the old-time characteristics of the past. Peanuts still are piled high on the corner stands, and the lemonade that is red tempts the thirsty at every step.

The asthmatic band of the flying horse tents still vexes the patient ear, and the side shows reap a harvest always.

From the Lancaster *Daily Examiner* of May 17, 1875.
Today, being Whit-Monday, the peculiar local manner of celebrating it was observed in the good old way, and our "country cousins" flocked in by rail and every conceivable style of vehicle, while many, within easy distance, walked in.

At an early hour the hotels and hotel stables in every part of the city were completely surrounded by vehicles, the streets were crowded uncomfortably for two or three squares from the centre in all directions; the curbs of the principal streets were lined with peanut and raspberry ade venders; the flying-horses held high carnival on East King Street, above Shippen; many of our merchants had their business wagons running in every direction with gaily caparisoned horses with bells on their necks;—all told that it was Whit-Monday, the great holiday peculiar to certain counties in Pennsylvania. There was no mistaking *that* fact—it was Whit-Monday! The merry songs of the curbstone venders of "good things" told it, the sparkling eyes of the rosy-cheeked country maidens told it, the ringing laughter of the town boys told it; the very bells *toll-ed* it, and we regret to say, the *unsteady* steps of many of the sterner sex, young and old, told it.

From the Lancaster *New Era* of June 2, 1884.
They [the people] were not in the usual numbers, the crowd being much less than that of former years. This is due, partly, to the fact that there are no longer any special attractions in this city on Whit-Monday.

And yet there were a good many people in the city. Just what they came for is a mystery; just what they *have* been coming for, for some years past, is equally a mystery. Time was when we had circuses, museums, flying-horses, minstrels on wagons, grotesque figures and all that sort of thing to please the young and even to attract the attention of the old; now there are absolutely no attractions—at least not such as to warrant coming a considerable distance, at no inconsiderable expense, to see the fair of the Reynolds Rifles at their armory, East King Street, the picnic of Taylor's Orchestra and a couple of other picnics of lesser degree of interest—these were all. A drum corps, advertising a business house, gave some life to the town, but otherwise the day was dull. Hundreds of people stood listlessly watching the workmen on the new street railway, and now and then the monotony was broken by the yell of some rustic who had taken too much colored lemonade. It was *not* the olden time Whit-Monday, and we regret to say it. Beneficial, or the reverse, Whit-Monday and its peculiar observance was an "institution" in this county—always honored more for its age than for its beauty—but now that its glory has departed would it not be as well to lay it peacefully to rest and sing a requiem over its grave?

HUMMEL BYERLIP'S WHITMONDAY

This account of Whitsuntide in Lancaster County in the opening decades of the nineteenth century is from the pen of James N. Beck (1828–1885), a Lititz native. It is from the Philadelphia *Evening Bulletin* of 1858. To fully understand this "short story" it must be understood that its author was a Moravian, a denomination whose membership has from Colonial days on felt itself "above" the folk culture of rural Pennsylvania Dutchland.

'Twas the Saturday eve before Whitsuntide. Hummel Byerlip wiped the dripping perspiration from his bronzed forehead, replaced the spotted cotton handkerchief into his plain straw hat, shouldered his axe, and muttered to himself as he cast his eyes toward the turnpike highway, which leads from the city of Lancaster northward "*Dort gayt die Litizer stage; sell ish mei uhr; yets muss es nacht esse faertig sei.*" (There goes the Lititz stage; that is my watch; now supper must be ready.) For two lonely hours had Hummel hacked perseveringly away at an ancient chestnut tree of colossal proportions, which stood in the centre of one of his sire's grain fields, and which, now that

extreme age had dried its vitality, had been deemed by the men upon the farm merely a serious obstacle to their ploughing operations, radiating beneath the soil, as it did, its tough and sinuous roots, for many yards around.

When the hoary old tree had fallen with a sharp crack and a ponderous crash, with the final stroke of the glittering axe, Hummel Byerlip had surveyed its prostrate trunk with a sense of relief and of self-glorification, such as Hercules may have experienced, when, in the cause of his Olympian father, his trusty club had felled to earth some gigantic conspirator of the Cottus, Briareus and Gyges rebellion; and then the weary laborer, as above mentioned, turned his steps homeward.

Crossing the fields at slow pace, Hummel reached the farm-house just as the call for supper had assembled the women and men around the amply stocked board; and his father, drawing out the ancient silver time keeper, muttered "*Bischt a wenig shpayter ols immer, Hummel.*" (You are a little later than always, Hummel.)

"*Sis kay wunner,*" rejoined the son, "*wen mer so a zayer shtick flaysh wie seller bohm zu schneide hut; er wor so hort wie a kloumpe pigeise.*" (No wonder, when one has to cut a piece of meat so tough as that tree; it was as hard as a lump of pig iron.)

During the meal, the conversation turned mainly upon the annual holiday recreation of Whit-monday, now so closely at hand, and the pater familias inquired of the men, "*Well von eich gayt nei nach Lengeshter iwer morge?*" (Which of you is going to Lancaster day after to-morrow?) In response whereto he noticed an assenting nod of head of each participant of the supper.

"*Es gebt widder grossy zeite drin,*" proceeded the sire of Hummel Byerlip, "*sie ben doe hunne in Neffsville g'sawed es soll a orig gross show—tieger, offe, komayle un so—gewe.*" (There will be a great time in town again; they said down in Neffsville, that there is to be a great show there—tigers, apes, camels, &c.)

When Hummel had finished his repast, he quickly ascended the stairway, which led to his contracted sleeping apartment, opened a closet which stood near the top-most step, and drew therefrom a pair of yellow nankeen trowsers, a vest of the same color and texture, and finally a dark tweed sack coat, with which articles of summer apparel he proceeded forthwith to array his hardy frame.

Stepping for an instant to the stunted garret window, he called forth to a cowboy in the yard beneath, *"Henner, fitter g'schwind mei schworzi maer!"* (Henry, feed my black mare quickly!) *"Don shpon sie ei; es komt boll e g'witter; ich mus mich shicke wen ich fort komme soll."* (Then hitch her up; there is a thunder storm coming; I must hurry, if I am to get off.)

Then hastened he to complete his rustic toilet; and at the end of an hour, Hummel might have been perceived driving rapidly along a by-road, westwardly from his paternal domains. The atmosphere was oppressively sultry, and the distant horizon lined with huge strata of pitchy clouds, while far-off rumblings of thunder and occasional fitful coruscations of heat lightning seemed like the fearful evidences which bring to the marching soldier the consciousness of an approaching conflict. Hummel's spirited black mare trotted briskly along, raising a dense cloud of dust with each rapid step of her agile limbs, and at the end of the fourth mile from home, deposited her driver at the door of Hannah Krumbach's neat residence. *"Bischt ziemlish hort g'fawre!"* said the father of the girl to our hero, who had stepped forward to greet his son-in-law in prospectu, *"soll ich ous-shponne?"* (You have driven pretty hard; shall I unhitch?) Hummel alleged that it would be impossible to remain all night as was his wont, owing to a promise he had made to his mother and sisters to accompany them to the house of a friend in the vicinity of Hammer Creek, on the following day; but he averred his intention to return to the house of his future father-in-law on the evening of the morrow, when he proposed to remain over-night, with a view to take Hannah into Lancaster on the following morning, in order to participate with her in the holiday sports of Whitmonday.

In pursuance thereof, old Krumbach contented himself with merely leading the foaming mare under the cover of an antiquated wagon shed; while Hummel stalked lumberingly into the kitchen, where stood his inamorata, rinsing the milk pans, in total unconsciousness of his arrival. She was humming a rude couplet, as the monotonous moments flew by; and when Hummel heard the strain, he halted in the passage way to discover its purport.

Der Hummel komt, der Hummel komt,
Dess dreibt mer alles schmaerz,
Der Hummel komt, der Hummel komt
Ess siss mer gut ums haerz!

[Hummel is coming, Hummel is coming,
This drives all my grief away.
Hummel is coming, Hummel is coming,
I feel so good about it!]

The subject of the rustic refrain waited for no repetition thereof, but called to her, with a broad leer upon his hardy features, *"Hannah, waer hot dir sell gelaernt?"* (Hannah, who taught you that?) Whereat the girl, surprised beyond measure not to have noticed the entrance of her lover, dropped her milk pans, and having wiped her soaked hands upon a rough towel which hung aside of the fireplace, hastened across the kitchen toward Hummel, who had now seated himself upon a low three legged stool, and jumping into his lap kissed him and replied *"Sell hov ich selver ous-shtudirt."* (That I studied out myself.)

Hummel Byerlip remained with the ruddy Hannah Krumbach until the hour of ten—when the storm, which had muttered and rumbled in the distance, during the entire evening, seemed gradually approaching nearer and nearer to that section of the country. Old Krumbach, whose reliability as a weather prophet had never been questioned by the surrounding country folk, had declared for the sixth time, after watching the inky clouds, as the more threatening bulk of these capriciously veered now Northward and then into the opposite direction, fluctuating between divers counter-currents of air, *"Ich will gut d'vor sei doss ess nett do haer komt."* (I will guarantee that it will not come here.) But the confident farmer's prediction was doomed to falsification, inasmuch as there arose without at the conclusion of his assertion, a sudden whirlwind, which violently slammed and banged the loose shutters, and drove into the open door of the kitchen a copious volley of moist green leaves from garden trees outside.

Then there ensued a temporary lull, during which old Krumbach made another meteorological observation, and returned with his opinions somewhat modified, declaring that the thunderstorm might reach that part of the country after all, but gave it as his opinion that the rain would scarcely commence in earnest for some hours; for proceeded he, "*Der poohohn greischt mer noch nett lout g'nug.*" (The peacock does not scream loud enough as yet.)

Hummel, who was accustomed to regard the sire of his betrothed as an infallible oracle, jumped from his seat, and declared his intention to make a strenuous effort to reach home before the lowering storm should break. To bid his hospitable entertainers good night, and to jump into his light buggy required but the space of a few moments; and ere long found he the candle lights of the farm house to have disappeared behind an adjacent hillock. Directing the course of his willing mare toward the highway which leads from Lancaster to the peaceful Moravian village of Lititz, Hummel pondered with joyful anticipation upon the coming *Pingsht-montag* (Whitmonday) and its concomitant sports. Suddenly his favorite mare stopped in mid-career, so abruptly indeed as to throw him forcibly against the dash board of the vehicle. She must have been frightened by a clap of thunder, which a moment before had disturbed the night with a tremendous boom, reasoned Hummel within himself, surprised at a freak of the beast which the latter had never exhibited before. But when the ordinarily well trained mare peremptorily refused to stir from the spot, in spite of all his commands or caresses, Hummel bethought him that there must be something unnatural upon the highway, which his human eyesight failed to perceive.

The mare trembled moreover, and pawed the ground with terrified vehemence; and while her master vainly essayed to guess the cause of her unnatural perturbation, the rain commenced to fall with floodlike vehemence. Peal after peal of thunder rolled along the darkened heavens, while ever and anon a vivid flash of lightning illumed the dreary scene, lighting up for a moment the surrounding landscape, and disclosing to the farm boy's view his dripping mare, standing amid the same symptoms of trepidation. Hummel was ignorant, and equally superstitious with others of his class. Frightened by a thunderstorm?—not he; but a strange feeling of terror crept through his hardy frame, when the idea flashed across his mind, that something supernatural must be exercising its influence upon his mare. Presently he heard unearthly voices,

seemingly a short distance off, voices shouting hoi! hoi! hoi! or some strange interjections akin to these. *Horrible dictu!* A vivid flash of lightning at that instant revealed to the terrified Hummel an apparition of such monstrous calibre and unnatural form, as caused his hair to rise on end, and his eyes to roll wildly in their sockets. The mare reared once, then kicked violently; and her master dropped the reins from his hands just in time to save himself from being dragged forward, when she tore the shafts from the main body of the vehicle, and ran from the spot with frightful rapidity.

Hummel Byerlip leaped from the conveyance at the moment when the violent wrench of the beast freed herself, and overturned it. Confused and giddy, stood he in the road for an instant, until another flash of the electric agent revealed the monstrous apparition again, and in close proximity with his person. To him the terrifying object seemed larger than his father's farm house, with huge flapping ears, and a curling nose fully six feet in length. Unnatural, hoarse voices, too, cursing frightful oaths, seemed goading the hideous, leviathan spectre onward to his destruction—and Hummel, drenched to the skin, sick with fright, sank down speechless and inanimate upon the roadside.

When returning consciousness reopened his eyes, the terrified Bushwacker discovered himself lying upon the saturated clover flowers of a field close to the scene of his nocturnal adventure. Judge of his joy to find that the hideous monster had disappeared and that the thunderstorm had given place to a bright sky, wherein the twinkling stars seemed to shine more lustrously than ever, after the gloom which has temporarily extinguished their lights. There lay his mutilated buggy in the position into which his mare had flung it; but he vainly addled his brains in the attempt to account for his transferment from the highway into the clover patch.

At that instant, a light as of a covered lantern beamed from the woods down below, and a voice crying Hummel Byerlip! Hummel Byerlip! broke the solemn stillness of the night. Hummel recognized the call of his father's cow-boy with joyfulness, and sprang eagerly forward to greet a friendly face in his distress.

"*In oller welt, Henner, woe ish mei maer?*" (In all the world, where is my mare?) shouted he, when the lantern and its carrier had reached him.

"*Im shtoll!*" quoth the latter, "*sie ish allaynig naw house komme, awer wo bish du gebliewe?*" (In the stable! She came home alone, but where have you stayed?)

"*Sis mer ferflucht kroum gange*" (It has gone cursedly crooked with me), said the excited Hummel, "*ich hob a schrecklicher geischt gesay.*" (I have seen a terrible spirit.) "*Gouck doe sin noch die grosse shpoure,*" (See, here are still its large tracks) continued he, pointing to certain huge, but regular impressions in the mud—too immense to have been the marks of any natural living being.

Henner, the cowboy, marvelled at the patent evidence which substantiated the correctness of his master's assertions about the "*geischt*"; then assuring him of his unfeigned joy at finding him unharmed, he proceeded on the way down to the farm, to recount how the mare had come directly home—and how he, frightened by the nonappearance of his master, had hurried out, as soon as he had been able to dress himself, in order to secure the mare, and to extend his assistance to the mysteriously missing Hummel.

The latter, after reaching his home, threw himself upon an uneasy and sleepless bed. His mind seemed totally distraught by the events which had transpired. Even when a lull in his excited fancies allowed him a momentary doze, his transient sleep was harassed with towering phantoms, monstrous shapeless forms, with an infinitude of long curling noses and flapping ears.

Soon, however, day broke; and the rising sun ushered in one of the loveliest of Sabbath morns. When Hummel came to the breakfast table, his father seemed surprised to find him there, accustomed as was the son to stop over night at Krumbach's.

"*Woss bringt dich zu hous? Und du sayscht aw so bloss ous—woss faylt, Hummel?*" (What brings you to the house? And you look so pale—what's the matter with you, Hummel?) quoth the father.

"*Ich hob a geischt gesay!*" (I saw a ghost) replied the hero of our sketch; and then narrated he the events to his wondering sire, just as they had transpired.

One of the farm hands sneered at Hummel's description of the monster ghost, and chucklingly remarked, "*Ess waerd wohl em Youckel Gans sei browner bull gewayse sei!*" (It was probably Yockle Gans's brown bull!)

"*Ferfluchter Aesel!*" thundered the narrator, "*denkscht du ich dayt a geischt net vom a bull kenne!*" (Cursed Ass! don't you think I should know a bull from a spirit?) "*Gayt amole nous uf 'em Lengeshterer waig un sayt amole die shpoure!*" (Go out into the Lancaster road and see the tracks!)

The caviller at Hummel's story uttered not another sneering word; and the entire "*householtung*" marvelled at the adventure which had befallen the hero of this sketch. Soon indeed did the narrative become circulated in every farmhouse through the vicinity; and old Krumbach, with his daughter Hannah, came driving over to the Byerlips to assure themselves, from personal observation, of Hummel's safety.

Speculation as to the true nature of the unnatural monster seemed to mystify the farmers in an increased proportion; and all the theories set agog merely served to imbue them more firmly with their absurd faith in the existence of ghosts.

On the following Monday morn, Hummel Byerlip and his inamorata drove out of the farm yard of the Krumbachs', and took the road to Lancaster. The black mare trotted briskly along in the cool matinal breeze, and the highway seemed filled to repletion with Bushwhacker, in every conceivable form of country conveyance, on horseback, and on foot, all tending in a southerly direction toward the holiday sports of Whitmonday. Forsooth it was a lovely morn. Birds chirped and fluttered in joyous gladness among the bushes and in every tree; flowers bloomed with diamond dew drops studding their tinted petals; bees hummed droningly amid the roses, which still hung drooping with the heaviness of the night moisture from their stems; and the cheery whistle of the cowboy, driving his cattle to the pasture, blended with the restive call of the male partridge to his fellow-brood.

Hummel's conversation with Hannah constantly reverted to the perilous adventure through which he had passed on the Saturday eve previous; and howbeit, urged by his betrothed to dismiss from his mind the unpleasant reminiscences connected therewith, he seemed to brood over them with racking mental efforts to solve the mystery. He alleged that the individual who had once encountered a "*geischt*" might be liable to another visitation from the same; and when the girl asked him "*warum?*" (why?) his reply was "*weils immer so ish*" (because it is always so); and cited the case in substantiation, of a certain Bill Kratzmaul, who had seen the spirit of a defunct militia captain some years before, and who from that time onward had received semi-annual visits from his spectral annoyer, until the grievance had driven him to sell his property, and migrate to distant parts, where his peace of mind might be less disturbed, *"und der geischt ish 'em nach"* (and the ghost followed him), said Hummel moodily, his countenance assuming a look of superstitious abstraction.

"Ken sei es wor doch kay geischt; seller wo du g'say hoscht!" (Could be it wasn't a ghost after all, what you saw!) interposed his sweetheart; but Byerlip flared up at the doubting tenor of her remark.

"Denkscht my maer waer weg g'schprunge?" (Do you think my mare would have run away?) *"Un wie bin ich iwer die fence komme, wie ich unmachtig wor?"* (And how did I get over the fence, when I had fainted?) *"Have ich kay age?"* (Have I no eyes?) *"Sog mer des oll, maedli!"* (Tell me all this, girl!)—thus spake Hummel, vexed that the perception of his senses should be questioned; and with that the twain entered North Queen St., Lancaster.

In a few moments more, the hero of our sketch had found accommodations for his mare, at a public house which seemed filled to repletion with country people from every portion of the country. The streets seemed swarming with these pleasure-seekers, who tramped heavily up and down the pavements, now staring vacantly into the shop windows, and anon watching with eager interest a mounted horse jockey—a dumpy, fat man, who rode a stout steed backward and forward before the constantly increasing throng, bawling aloud, "splendid draught horse—perfectly sound—trained to single and double harness—never kicks in the traces—who says ninety? going! going! going—" and he did go, to the other end of the street, in search of a better bid.

Hundreds of the unsophisticated farmers stood around the railway depot, watching the arrival and departure of the morning trains; and gazing upon the begrimed engineers with feelings of awe and respect, as these stood upon their locomotives wiping the perspiration and ashes from their faces. Crowds flocked to a four story brick building over the way, whereon were affixed huge letters to spell the word "Museum," and from

whence issued unceasingly the sounds of a parlor organ, upon which a hired performer executed such morceaux as served to attract more readily the attention of the amusement-seeking Bushwhackers. Cake and peanut women drove a most flourishing business, retailing enormous slices of gingerbread to the rustic beaux, who gulped them in until their well filled mouths caused their cheeks to protrude like globes; and a superannuated colored individual, who had improvised an oyster stand in the Center Square, found himself incessantly compelled to replenish with milk his constantly drained cans of smoking soup. Then a well disciplined and handsomely uniformed military company marched through the principal streets, to the martial music of the drum and fife—an immense sensation for the rustic carousers, surely, and one which claimed their undivided attention, until a sudden rush up North Queen Street attested the coming of the Menagerie caravan.

Hummel Byerlip and Hannah Krumbach missed this imposing feature of the Whit-Monday sports; for they had gone to visit the county prison, or *"presint,"* as the former termed the public building in question. After leaving the gloomy receptacle, the two lovers tramped through the streets, hand in hand, surveying the tastefully arranged shop-windows, consuming large quantities of peanuts, and affording with hundreds of their class, an infinite quota of amusement to the educated citizens of the time-honored town.

"Witt aw in die show?" (Do you wish to go to the show too?) queried Hummel, after the pedestrians were seen wending their way enthusiastically along East King Street toward an open lot, where towered above the lowly houses surrounding, the octagonal menagerie tent.

"Worum den nett?" (Why not?) replied Hannah; *"ich hob noch sei laewe kay show g'sayne"* (I have never in my life seen a show). Neither had her rustic cavalier, whose impressions of the internal features of a menagerie were exceedingly vague and undefined. He had never even witnessed the toy-book picture of an ape, or a tiger—and as for an elephant or a hyena, the very names of these were as fully unknown to him as the Hydra of ancient mythology. Had Hummel passed into the respective bar rooms of Lancaster, in lieu of strolling through its crowded streets, the gorgeous menagerie posters

might have furnished him with an antepast of the surprising treat which the flabby tent at the upper end of East King Street held in store for him; but as it was, the twain wedged into the pavilion at the appointed time with mouths and eyes agape, and came upon the Royal Bengal Tiger at first glance.

"*Woss a immer un ewige grosse kotz!*" (What an ever and eternally big cat) ejaculated Hummel, recoiling a step to the rear as the hirsute keeper plied a raw hide vigorously through the bars of the cage, causing the ferocious beast to flash furiously from its eyes, and pirouette wildly around in its contracted receptacle.

"This," quoth the attendant, after a few final lashes which drove the enraged brute, growling and crouching, into a corner; "this is the Royal Bengal Tiger—found in the desolate thickets of Asia and Africa—and possessing the strength to bear away upon his fore-shoulders a full sized bullock. (Taking out his watch) "We shall feed him upon a live sheep at three o'clock precisely!"

Hummel, who comprehended not a syllable of the keeper's stereotyped speech, nudged his inamorata to follow him; and the denizens of each succeeding wagon cage—zebras, lions, wolves, gnus, hyenas, baboons, panthers, not to forget the graceful stag, "presented to the managers by her Majesty, Queen Victoria," and which is inseparable from every itinerant exhibition of the kind—were scrutinized by the unsophisticated couple with an increasing astonishment depicted upon their blunt features, which afforded infinite amusement to more refined lookers on.

Standing by the cage of a score of imprisoned but cheerfully chattering monkeys, Hummel and Hannah burst into an uproarious guffaw, which drew the attention of many bystanders, as they watched the antics of the mischievous pugs within, and noted the ludicrous facial similarity between these, and suddenly Hannah Krumbach turned about. A huge, ponderous, leaden-colored animal, with small eyes and immense flapping ears, stood oscillating from side to side, near the spot where they then found themselves. A man leaned against the fore-leg of the beast. He was dressed in the Hindoo costume, which, with his sunburnt features, gave him the genuine oriental aspect—and verily so truthful were his theatrical equipments, that e'en many of the

more educated visitors to the menagerie might have deemed him a veritable importation, but that his penchant for whittling stray chips with a pen-knife attested unmistakably his Yankee lineage.

Hannah felt frightened to encounter so monstrous an animal as the elephant, Tippoo Saib, uncaged and apparently at liberty to stalk forth at option, into the dense mass of people.

"Hummel," said she, squeezing the arm of her lover, who still gazed with unabated merriment into the cage of monkeys, somewhat timidly, "*woss ish sell gross ding dort?*" (What is that big thing there?)

The Bushwhacker turned abruptly around to see for himself; and with that instant an ashy paleness overcame his features, as he muttered between his chattering teeth, while his limbs trembled with sudden fright, "*So wor ich layb, doe ish widder mei geischt.*" (So sure as I live, here is my ghost again.) Many persons, noticing his extreme agitation, immediately sought to know what might be the cause of this sudden perturbation; and the Hindoo keeper, perceiving the sensation in the crowd, leaped over the ropes which hemmed his elephant into a suitable enclosure, and mingled curiously with the pressing throng. Hummel pushed to the right and to the left, in the vain effort to force an egress through the rapidly accumulating crowd; and the bystanders deemed him distraught when he called out frantically, "*Losst mich naw hous—der geischt komt mer widder nach!*" (Let me go home—the ghost is after me again!) At that instant, the sagacious Tippoo Saib, discovering the absence of his keeper, stalked majestically forward, after pulling up the stakes and ropes of his pen with one wrench of his trunk. A scene of inextricable confusion ensued, during which people fled into all directions, pushing, shoving, kicking, and trampling with the ruthless vehemence of a panic-stricken multitude. Women and children screamed wildly, men swore, the animals bewildered by the noisy melee, vented uneasy growls—while the elephant moved slowly and harmlessly onward, until he came to the spot where Hummel Byerlip and Hannah Krumbach were even then vainly essaying to discover a place of security by creeping under the leopard cage. The noble animal halted before the terrified lovers, looking sagaciously at them, as though conscious of Hummel's agency in the origin of the disturbance while anon stretched he his trunk under the wagon, seemingly with an intention to drag them from their place of secretion.

At this moment, just as the individual guardians of the menagerie had succeeded in pacifying the terrified crowd, forth stepped the Hindoo keeper of the gigantic Tippoo, and taking hold of the animal's ears, quietly led him back to his proper position. Having berated the beast for the breach of discipline of which the latter had shown himself guilty, the man hastened back to the leopard's cage, and peering between the wheels, called to the terrified Hummel and his companion to come forward, assuring them that all danger had passed; and when the superstitious young Bushwhacker ventured forward, the keeper, after scanning him closely for an instant, burst forth into a boisterous guffaw, exclaiming to a showman near him:

"Why Jake, this is the same man the elephant picked out of the mud the other night, when we were driving him to town; I'm darned if it ain't. I know him by his nankeen breeches and by the painted red star on the crown of his straw hat. Tippoo knew him too, and that's what brought the animal away from his stand into the crowd." Then turning to Hummel he continued, "Did you ever get your mare back, Dutchman? My eyes! how scientifically the elephant lifted you out of the street, and laid you in the clover patch! What a tarnation shrewd animal."

Hummel comprehended not a syllable of the interjections, which, if he had possessed even a limited knowledge of English, might have explained to him the most mysterious feature of his Saturday night's adventure, viz.: his unaccountable transferment from the road into the field.

The bystanders, who had crowded around in dense numbers, tittered to perceive the mystified expression which the countenance of our hero now wore, and many sneeringly remarked, "*Du hoscht anyhow dei faertel tawler waert grickt*" (you have received your quarter's worth, at all events), while Hummel, no longer in a fitting mood to pursue his first lesson in Natural History, seized the hand of his sweetheart, and stalked out of the arena, dragging her after him, just as the crowd shuffled and wedged around the inner circle to witness the amusing evolutions and trained performances of a grimacing monkey, arrayed in a scarlet coat and cap, and a jetblack shetland pony, led in at that moment.

It was a long time after the return of Hummel Byerlip and Hannah Krumbach from the Whit-monday in Lancaster, before people succeeded in effectually laughing and ridiculing away the preposterously superstitious belief concerning the elephant, which had fastened itself so deeply upon the unsophisticated mind of our hero. However, a few winter sessions of tuition at a neighboring boarding school of marked celebrity, where Hummel, apart from the ordinary study of rudimental branches, enjoyed the benefits of a course of lectures upon Natural Philosophy, Chemistry, Zoology and divers other scientific subjects, wrought a marvellous change within the subject of the present sketch; and when, in after years, Hummel found himself comfortably situated upon the estate of his late father, he was wont to relate, with much gusto, to his numerous brood of youthful Byerlips, the events herein related, describing in a joking manner the festivities of the Whit-monday in Lancaster, which had afforded him a glimpse of the elephant under circumstances thus strange and novel.

Afterword

Eastertide in Pennsylvania (1960), with its precise and dated ethnographic detail on the full range of Pennsylvania Dutch holiday customs from the eighteenth, nineteenth, and early twentieth centuries, is a major contribution to American folklife studies. The national resonance produced by his earlier holiday study, *Christmas in Pennsylvania* (1959), inspired Alfred Shoemaker to put into readable book form all of his earlier articles on the subject of spring holidays—from Shrove Tuesday to Pentecost—which had appeared in the journal of the Pennsylvania Dutch Folklore Center, *The Pennsylvania Dutchman*.

What makes this and the Christmas book unique in American research is Shoemaker's European-inspired research technique, which combined comprehensive historical documentation (nineteenth- and early twentieth-century newspapers, biographical data, dialect materials, and even short stories) with the wide-ranging ethnographic interviews he performed all over the Dutch Country. Whenever he met true "tradition bearers," as folklorists and anthropologists describe persons who grow up within a culture and have a memory full of the details of how that culture operated, he interviewed them, carefully jotting down their information, including Pennsylvania Dutch dialect expressions and vocabulary. Like *Christmas in Pennsylvania*, this volume is a model of painstaking ethnographic research, historical as well as current, and deserves the compliment of imitation in other cultural areas and ethnic enclaves of the United States.

Ethnography, as originally conceived by anthropologists, entails descriptive reporting—as in this book—on one particular culture, or on specific aspects of that culture. Its purpose is not to analyze or theorize underlying meanings, functions, or purposes of the cultural traits it describes. Hence to complete Alfred Shoemaker's unmatched descriptions of the springtime holidays in our Dutch Country, I propose in this afterword to summarize some of the analytical research that has been done on festival customs and their meanings, in both European and American scholarship. Rather than ranging over the entire field of spring holiday research, however, I shall focus my discussion on Fastnacht and Easter.

When comparing Shoemaker's ethnographic record of the spring holiday calendar of the Pennsylvania Dutch with the European regional research on the same subject, it appears that the Pennsylvania customs are somewhat attenuated and migratory. By attenuated I mean that not all the riches of the European festival year were able to be transplanted across the Atlantic. Indeed, some traditions were attenuated in Europe even before the emigration to Pennsylvania, Protestant forces having attacked, downgraded, and destroyed some, but not all, of our ancestral festival customs.

By migratory I suggest that certain customs, for reasons that are not always easy to explain, have migrated from the holiday with which they were associated in Europe, to other days in the festival calendar. The best example of this phenomenon is the European custom of processions and house-rounds by masked adults and youth at Fastnacht, which, transplanted in Pennsylvania, emerged as the processions and house-rounds of masked Bels-nickels or fantasticals at Christmas, New Year's, and other holidays. The reason can be partially found in the downgrading of Fastnacht by Protestantism. With the Lenten fast abrogated, there was no real reason for the celebratory and compensatory aspects of Fastnacht to continue their existence. The people, however, who enjoyed masking, masquerading, street processions, house visits, and general revelry simply transferred their celebrations to such permitted holidays as Christmas and New Year's Day.

In Europe there was a strong differential between festival customs as practiced in Catholic and Protestant areas. The Protestant Reformation of the sixteenth century, and its further development into Puritanism, Pietism, and Evangelicalism in the seventeenth, eighteenth, and nineteenth centuries, put its sometimes negative stamp on the Catholic church year and its festival customs. The major biblical holidays—Christmas, Easter, Ascension Day, and Pentecost—were retained, but the rich pattern of nonbiblical saints' days of medieval Catholicism was officially dropped by the church. Many of the customs and beliefs associated with these Catholic days, however, went "underground," as Alfred Shoemaker put it, and continued to be practiced in the Protestant European and Pennsylvania Dutch folk cultures.

FOLK RELIGION, FOLK SPIRITUALITY

In European folk culture and in primitive culture as well, our ancestors had a different sense of the sacred, and they divided the world into sacred and secular components differently than most of us do today. In European peasant societies, the community to which everybody belonged was sacred. The church and the cemetery were sacred space, separate from the secular space surrounding them. The house was also sacred space, oriented to the sun and blessed when erected. Even in Pennsylvania our earlier farmhouses had date-

stones that pronounced blessings on those who dwelt within.

What was true of our ancestors' sense of space was also true of their sense of time, which they divided into everyday (secular) and festival (sacred) aspects. Certain times in human life were also sacred, especially the so-called rites of passage, when an individual was ritually moved forward out of his old peer group in the folk community into a new higher group. This movement happens, for example, with marriage, when the bride and groom leave the ranks of unmarried youth and join the housefathers and matrons in their community, with new duties and responsibilities.

Ethnographers call the sacred times in the calendar "festivals of the year." These can be based either on the agricultural or seasonal year, or on the church year. Christmas, Easter, Ascension Day, Pentecost, and others, are prescribed by the church. But although these days and times have an ecclesiastical core, through the centuries the people have embroidered them with extra-ecclesiastical festivities and frills like the Christmas tree, the Easter egg, the Easter rabbit, Whitsun fairs, and shooting in the New Year. Some of these popular enjoyments can claim lineages equally as long as, if not longer than, those of the properly Christian celebrations of the churches. Many of these customs were, at least in earlier stages of our ancestral cultures, frankly pagan, survivals or retentions from pre-Christian stages of human spirituality. In some cases these customs were tolerantly embraced or manipulated by the church; in others they were forbidden, tabooed, outlawed. For the official church, it has been a long battle to combat these delightful pagan customs through the centuries. And in the case of many of these activities and the beliefs once associated with them, the church has fought a losing battle.

What happened beginning with the Reformation was a separation of religion into two somewhat conflicting forces: the official religion of the Protestant churches with their educated clergy, theological orthodoxy, and formal liturgies; and a folk or people's religion much broader in range than the official religion of church services, sermons, hymnbooks, and catechisms. For this broader type of religion among the people, we can use the term *folk religion* or *folk spirituality*. By these terms we mean forms of religious belief and practice that were not always approved by the official church organizations, but were in some cases tolerated and thus have continued to the present generation.

Pennsylvania Dutch folk spirituality included a vast body of beliefs and practices associated with the major Christian holidays—those accepted by official Protestantism—and the minor saints' days and seasonal festivals that had come down from the Catholic Middle Ages. As Alfred Shoemaker often pointed out in his lectures and writings, whereas the *official* religion of the Pennsylvania Dutch was almost entirely Protestant, the *folk* religion was essentially Catholic and medieval in content. The Pennsylvania Dutch folk culture, with its large contingent of folk spirituality and its double provenance of official and folk religion, is thus one of the richest, most fascinating subcultures in America. It is even more compelling when we remember that this great range of pre-Protestant folk custom was brought over to Pennsylvania not in written form but in the memories and hearts of our emigrant ancestors who crossed the Atlantic in the seventeenth, eighteenth, and early nineteenth centuries.

EUROPEAN SCHOLARSHIP AND SEASONAL CUSTOMS

The history of folk-cultural research in Europe and America is, like the history of any academic discipline, extremely complex, and we can here only sample a few trends that affected American holiday research. Early American folklore research was largely derivative of the comparative folklore or comparative mythology approach used by English folklorists. After the founding of the British Folklore Society (1878) and the American Folklore Society (1888), scholars scoured the world for customs similar to traditional English ones, and comparative folklore was born. This approach relates similar customs, festivals, and so forth, from all over the world, to the customs, festivals, and beliefs one is researching, whether or not they have any organic, historical, or evolutionary relation to each other. The great monument of this approach in British Isles scholarship is Sir James G. Frazer's twelve-volume work, *The Golden Bough: A Study in Magic and Religion* (1911–1915).

Actually, much continental European folk-cultural scholarship had preceded the English discovery of folklore, a term coined in 1846. As early as 1788 German scholars were using the term *Volkskunde* for the study of the "folk" and its customs. It was joined by the term *Volksleben*, which became *folkliv* in Swedish and *folklife* as adapted in Great Britain and Ireland and transferred to Pennsylvania by Alfred Shoemaker and our joint Pennsylvania Dutch Folklore Center and its successor, the Pennsylvania Folklife Society.

Of the many contributions of *Volkskunde* to German and international scholarship, let us look briefly at *Deutsche Mythologie* (*German Mythology*), a work by the prolific Germanist Jacob Grimm (1785–1863), published in 1835. A four-volume English edition (1883–1888) was translated by English scholar James Steven Stallybrass. Unfortunately for American readers, although Stallybrass translated Grimm's German text, he left untranslated Grimm's many direct quotations from Greek and Latin, since he expected his classically trained English readers to be able to read them at sight. Also, to reflect Grimm's wide-ranging materials from Scandinavian and other related sources,

Stallybrass renamed the work *Teutonic Mythology*. Dover Publications in New York issued the Stallybrass translation for the American public in 1966.

Grimm's work is still indispensable for understanding the ancient traditional backgrounds of German folk culture, including the holidays and beliefs and practices associated with them. Easter, for example, the first great church festival of Christianity to develop, has pagan roots. In its official religious dimension, Easter commemorates the passion, death, and resurrection of Christ. To our pagan ancestors in northern Europe, long before there was an organized Christian religion, the time of Easter was also sacred. It was a spring festival, the central one in fact, which celebrated the death of winter and the rebirth of vegetation and, in a sense, of life itself. It is significant that when pagans were converted to Christianity in Germanic northern Europe and in England, the Church retained for the new Christian holiday the pagan name "Easter." Christmas, incidentally, is a relative newcomer compared with Easter; it was not until the fourth century A.D. that December 25—then a major pagan holiday celebrating the birthday of the Invincible Sun (*Sol Invictus*)—was chosen and retreaded by church authorities into a Christian festival.

EUROPEAN ROOTS OF THE EASTER FESTIVAL

Grimm gave us his reasoned thoughts on the origin of the name of our Easter festival: The Venerable Bede, in his history of the Anglo-Saxon people and the origins of their Christian faith in England, mentions an ancient goddess named *Eastre* or *Eostra*, from whom the Anglo-Saxons took their name for April, *Esturmonath*, or "Easter month." Since still in Grimm's day the Germans called April *Ostermonat*, a term documented as far back as Charlemagne's time, around 800 A.D., Grimm saw no reason to doubt Bede's ascription.

In modern German the Christian festival of Easter is called *Ostern*, a plural word because (as in Pennsylvania) two days of celebration were involved, Easter Sunday and Easter Monday. The ancient Germanic term *Ostara*, like the Anglo-Saxon *Easter*, writes Grimm, "must in the heathen religion have denoted a higher being, whose worship was so firmly rooted, that the Christian teachers tolerated the name, and applied it to one of their own grandest anniversaries." All the nations surrounding Germany, however, retained the biblical word *pascha*, a term associated originally with the Jewish Passover.

Grimm's linguistic analysis becomes even more complicated, and fascinating. The Old High German word *Ostar* expresses movement toward the east, toward the rising sun. Hence, *Ostara/Eastre* appears "to have been the divinity of the radiant dawn, of upspringing light, a spectacle that brings joy and blessing, whose meaning could easily be adapted to the resurrection-day of the Christian's God." And there is more: "*Bonfires* were lighted at Easter, and according to a popular belief of long standing, the moment the sun rises on Easter Sunday morning, he gives *three joyful leaps*, he dances for joy." Also, "water drawn on the Easter morning is, like that at Christmas, holy and healing; hence also heathen notions seem to have grafted themselves on great Christian festivals."

Fires at Easter and Midsummer (St. John's Day, June 24) were transferred, Grimm suspects, from May Day. May 1 (like November 1, February 1, and August 1) was a cardinal turning point in the year for the ancient Celtic peoples, who lived in Germany before and in many cases at the same time as the Romans and invading Germanic tribes. November 1 was the Celtic New Year, the beginning of the first half of the "dark half of the year" (winter); February 1 began winter's second half; May 1 was the beginning of the first half of the "light half of the year" (summer); and August 1 began its second half. All of these turning points of the Celtic year were eventually grafted onto the Christian festival year as ecclesiastically determined holidays.

In pagan times ceremonial fires were lighted on these Celtic holidays, which were festivals of light and good fortune. Leaping over the fires brought health in the next time period; leading cattle between two fires brought protection, health, and fertility. Rolling a lighted wheel down the hills into the valleys strengthened the progress of the sun through the year. In some cases these customs came down far into Christian times. Grimm tells us that Easter fires were lighted on the hills above villages, and there was exuberant dancing and singing, with processions to the fire. Revelers sang Easter hymns and shouted hallelujahs, and in some areas carried some of the fire home with them. (In Celtic times on certain festival days, hearth fires were extinguished and then relit with coals from the communal fire.) Easter fires were more common in North Germany, in the Saxon territories, than in South Germany. Grimm also reports that in the last hundred years the celebratory fires lighted at Easter were forbidden by the local authorities. The older prohibitions, says Grimm, "allege the unchristian character, later ones the waste of timber!"

Because of *Deutsche Mythologie*, Grimm was considered the father of the science of comparative mythology in Europe. His work, based on his immense knowledge of European linguistics and classical and medieval literature, is still a standard reference work and has continued to influence scholarship in Germany and the rest of Europe, as well as America.

"GERMANIC CONTINUITY" OR PRESENT-DAY FOLKLIFE?

With Grimm's work as model, the great twentieth-century monument of comparative folk-cultural research is the ten-volume *Handwörterbuch des Deutschen Aberglaubens* (1927–1942). (A caveat on the title of this work is necessary here. The German term *Aberglaube*, usually translated as *superstition*, is no longer recognized as a German scientific concept, nor is superstition in English. Hence the word should be transmuted into the neutral, non-prejudicial term *folk belief* or *traditional belief*.) This standard work, edited by two distinguished Swiss scholars, presents materials on a wide range of German folk-cultural traits gathered from all over the Germanic cultural areas of central Europe. This was an improvement on the English comparative folklore approach, since it concentrated on areas settled by Germanic tribes in late antiquity and the early Middle Ages, but it was still comparative.

After the First World War, German folklife scholars turned away from research that traced pre-Christian, pagan Germanic (or Teutonic) "continuity" down to the present. The newer functionalist sociological and anthropological approaches focused on the peasant village as a community made up of various interacting human groups. Festivity, costumes, and other folk-cultural phenomena were analyzed from the community standpoint: What meaning and function did they have for the community in the past and, more importantly, today? In more recent decades the German folklife scholars, preferring to call themselves European ethnologists, have largely rejected the awkward and bias-laden term *folk*, replacing it with the neutral *group*. And while festival folklife research has continued, the study of "folklife of the present day" (*Gegenwartsvolkskunde*) and "urban folklife" (*Grosstadtvolkskunde*) have pushed to the foreground, leaving peasant village culture to sentimentalists and nostalgic journalists.

Some of our earlier students of Pennsylvania Dutch folk culture were at least moderately influenced by continuity theories, but fortunately without the racist overtones that developed in late-nine-teenth-century nationalistic German scholarship and culminated in Nazi propaganda. Particularly affected were early Germanists like Edwin M. Fogel (1874–1949) and Preston A. Barba (1883–1971), two principal founders of the Pennsylvania German Folklore Society in 1935. Fogel produced several key articles on Christmas and other holidays as cele-brated in Pennsylvania, and two major monographs: *Beliefs and Superstitions of the Pennsylvania Germans* (1915), with its hush-hush supplement on "sex" printed "for private distribution" without English translations(!); and *Proverbs of the Pennsylvania Ger-mans* (1929), which also had a privately distributed supplement. Both of these are useful for beliefs and sayings associated with our holidays, and both have been reprinted recently—with the supplements in fluent English translation.

Professor Barba, who headed the German Department at Muhlenberg College for many years and was the longtime editor of publications for the Pennsylvania German Folklore Society, researched tombstone art and the barn decorations known as "hex signs." In the first case he used some astrolog-ical explanations, and in the second he saw hex signs as the end of a long chain of sun symbolism originating in the pre-Christian "Northland."

One of the best examples of recent European custom and festival research is the epochal book by the late Ingeborg Weber-Kellermann of the Uni-versity of Marburg, entitled *Saure Wochen Frohe Feste* (1985). The title refers to the alternation between hard everyday work and joyous festival celebration. In this work the author gives a rational critique of present-day festival customs. She begins by telling the reader that many con-temporary festivals, even those in German villages, are actually either newly invented or revived from early stages of the local culture, when the commu-nity was still a social and psychological unit.

Today's festivals are increasingly put on for the tourists, who in turn help to swell the town's econ-omy. The festivals are often still touted in advertis-ing and the media as demonstrating Germanic cultic forms carried down from ancient times to the present. This, she says, is based on the pious hope that there was once an ideal human world in that distant, mythical past.

All of this, according to Weber-Kellermann, is secondhand, illusory, sentimental, and unrealistic. It represents an attempt to revivify long outmoded values. In "participating" in such events as an onlooker, the urban vacationer (tourist) hopes to find that lost "healthy world" among the costumed folk dancers in the half-timbered villages of pres-ent-day Germany. The village festival has become theater, with performers appearing from the wings to delight the audience.

In her biting but rational critique of these events, Professor Weber-Kellermann contends that old meanings and values, obviously out of date, have had to be replaced with new meanings and values for the current performance. One of her most con-vincing arguments against the continuity theory is her statement that in every village, even in the most remote valleys, the locals, and especially the youth among them, show no interest in history and have always longed to be modern, to reach the "fashion-able and civilizing modes of the present day."

These changes in festival content and meaning can be seen in America as well. What is today in America called a folk festival is very often a festi-val limited to folk music and folk dance. It involves not community participation as in the past, but entertainment staged for massive crowds, à la Woodstock and Schwenksville, through per-formances by folk singers, instrumentalists, and dancers. By contrast, in village festivals in the old valley communities of the Dutch Country, the Bels-nickels roamed; schoolmasters were barred out of schoolhouses by ingenious students; the local militia drilled at the crossroads tavern and stayed for a night of dancing, feasting, and drinking; and the farmer folk, eager for entertainment, invaded the county seats for the Whitsun or Cherry Fairs. In short, the entire community reveled.

FASTNACHT CUSTOMS IN GERMAN FOLK CULTURE

Let us now turn to the customs and beliefs associated with Fastnacht (Shrove Tuesday) in Germanic Europe, and then to their relevance to the Pennsylvania Dutch folk culture.

The comprehensive discussion of the meaning and functions of Fastnacht in Germanic folk culture in the *Handwörterbuch des Deutschen Aberglaubens* is a good place to start our analysis of the Pennsylvania evidence. This standard work makes fourteen points about European Fastnacht, which we shall summarize here.

1. Because the approaching forty-day fast of Lent is so long, Fastnacht is essentially a joyous holiday with permitted relaxation and frolic. Whereas the flashy big-city carnival parades of the Rhineland are no more than a century or two old, the village Fastnacht customs carry with them ancient traditions and the sense of ancient powers. In earlier times these powers were believed to impart to the increasing year fertility and blessing, while removing the danger posed by hostile powers in the universe.

2. Particularly joyous was the belief underlying many Fastnacht customs that by performing them we are helping to conquer winter and close out its long reign of cold and darkness. Fastnacht led the springtime in.

3. Fastnacht, like many holidays, encapsulated the idea that what one did on that day in house and garden would bring an especial blessing in the future. Fruit trees were often trimmed on this day to promote their bearing in the fruit harvest. If you greased the leather harnesses in the stables on Fastnacht, the draft animals would become strong and pull better the whole year. And lettuce sown on Fastnacht would yield abundantly.

4. Fastnacht was a preliminary spring housecleaning day, an act that would drive away vermin.

5. Winding straw around fruit trees on Fastnacht would increase their yield. Also, shaking the trees on this day imparted new life to them.

6. Farm animals, poultry, and cattle were protected from future harm by cleaning the chicken coop and other animal shelters, and by sticking birch branches in the barnyard. The cattle would rub against them and thus remain free from vermin.

7. Many traditional taboos or prohibitions accompanied these commands. Spinning, for example, was never done on Fastnacht, lest the flax crop turn out a failure that year. Whatever was spun on Fastnacht, the mice would find and eat. On this day spinning wheels and distaffs should be hidden or tied up. (Actually Candlemas—February 2—was the traditional end date for the winter spinning in Germanic Europe, and Pennsylvania as well, hence this curious set of ideas connects with Candlemas lore, too.)

8. Like other holidays, Fastnacht was a time when spirits and witches were abroad. This is why, according to some theorists, masks were worn on Fastnacht—to represent witches, the Devil, or hostile animals. Masks also protected the wearer from spirits of the dead that were revisiting the earth, the maskers being essentially disguised and therefore unrecognizable by the spirits. Noisemaking—also a popular component of the village Fastnacht celebration—was believed to scare away the evil powers that opposed fertility and to awaken and encourage the winter grain, thus warding off a bad harvest that summer.

9. Ritual fires, believed to consume evil and promote good, were lighted on Fastnacht, often on the

Masked Fastnacht revelers from the Black Forest in Germany. From Johannes Künzig, Die alemannisch-schwäbische Fasnet *(1950).*

hills around the village. In Canton Lucerne in Switzerland village neighbors reconciled with each other at these fires, and old animosities were believed to be consumed. Rolling burning wheels down the slopes into the valleys or striking wheels are ancient customs. They implied a sympathy with the sun, rolling through the heavens, and were thought to magically influence its growing power. Here we see Fastnacht's central role in the mythological conflict between winter and summer, darkness and light.

10. Striking or whipping animals, plants, or humans with the so-called *Lebensrute* (rod of life), a common Fastnacht custom, was believed to waken the seeds of fertility. Such rituals, for example, were thought to promise a good flax crop. In another effort to promote tall flax plants, farmers and their wives, and/or the young people of the village, danced and leaped in the fields—a classic case of imitative magic.

11. Because of the generally positive character of Fastnacht, the holiday season was a popular time for weddings, especially Fastnacht Monday.

12. In advance of the Lenten Fast on Ash Wednesday, Fastnacht was a time of feasting and drinking. Apart from the obvious pleasure this gave to our ancestors, such feasts were thought to betoken an abundant harvest. Leftovers were thought to contain special powers, so some were left for the angels, for the foxes, the hawks, and the martens.

13. Many cakes were baked on Fastnacht for mutual gift-giving. Fastnacht lard was employed as a wound salve and also used to grease plowshares and wagons before their first use in the spring fields.

14. Finally, like many other calendar dates, Fastnacht was a day of prophecy, a predictor of the weather or the summer harvest. If it snowed on Fastnacht, it would snow on Easter Sunday. If it froze on Fastnacht, flax would grow even on stone walls (i.e.,

it would be a good flax year). If icicles on the roof were long, the flax would grow tall (more imitative magic). And it is even more complex than that. As the weather was on Shrove Tuesday, so it would be in the hay harvest (the summer's first harvest); as it was on Ash Wednesday, so it would be in the grain harvest (the second harvest); and as it was on Thursday, so it would be in the *Grummeternte* (the harvesting of the second hay crop; note that the word *Grummet* is also the Pennsylvania Dutch expression for the second cutting of hay in the summer). And finally, more flax predictions: If the sun shone on Shrove Tuesday in the forenoon, flax would be planted early that year; if it did not shine until the afternoon, flax was to be planted late.

In analyzing this profusion of data, we have to point out that since this list of customs is comparative, gathered from all sections of the Germanic culture-world, not every region in Germanic Europe practiced *all* of them. It is surprising, however, how many of the beliefs and practices did make it across the Atlantic—transplanted here by generations of emigrants—and could be reported in the Dutch Country in the twentieth century, at least from older informants.

A few examples will suffice to prove this transatlantic continuance of Fastnacht customs. Since the European masking, processions, and Fastnacht house visitings were transferred to Christmas, New Year's, and other holidays. (see *Christmas in Pennsylvania*), the central practice of the Pennsylvania Shrove Tuesday holiday was the baking, giving, and eating of *Fastnachtkuchen*, translated fastnacht cakes or simply fastnachts. They are deep-fried cakes made of sweetened batter and further sweetened, when eaten, with powdered sugar, honey, or syrup, and can be circular, rectangular, or diamond shaped. They are still the favorite cakes in Pennsylvania for the Fastnacht season, so much so that many country and town churches now bake thousands of them for sale in their communities.

Because fastnachts are in a sense the product of a holy day, they are also credited with virtues beyond the nutritional. Fastnacht crumbs were fed to the chickens on Shrove Tuesday, for better egg laying, and also to protect them against the incursions of hawks. And leaving some for a visiting spirit or fairy brought good luck. Even the lard used in making fastnachts was used medically for healing sores and wounds, and magically for greasing wagons. Here it was not the plowshare that was greased before plowing the first spring field, but the spade before digging the garden. This was thought to keep insect pests from the summer vegetables.

Shrove Tuesday was also a high time for frolics, dances, and drinking parties at the local tavern or in the spacious farmhouses of the Dutch Country. Even the tavern dances were believed to affect the growth of the flax that year: The higher the couples leaped in the dance, the taller the flax plants would become. Flax was to our European and Pennsylvanian farmer ancestors a crucially important crop, since before the advent of cotton, the women of every family spent midwinter spinning flax to be woven into cloth for towels, sheets, shirts, and summer clothing. The European taboo against spinning on Shrove Tuesday was reflected among Pennsylvania farmers who prohibited sewing on that day.

One popular Pennsylvania Dutch Fastnacht custom—the bestowing of teasing names on the last person out of bed on Shrove Tuesday morning—is missing from the Fastnacht section of the *Handwörterbuch*, but appears in detail in the article on *Langschläfer* ("lie-abeds"). According to the *Wörterbuch der Deutschen Volkskunde* (1974), however, this custom is associated in Europe not only with Fastnacht but also with Ash Wednesday, Palm Sunday, Easter, May Day, Pentecost, certain

harvest times, and even New Year. In the past the last one sleeping on these days could receive a token beating with the *Lebensrute* to roust him out of bed, he could be sprinkled with water, ridiculed, made the subject of mocking verses, or given a nickname that sometimes went with him all year. The token beating was really not punitive, but was thought to bring growth, fertility, health, blessing, and happiness.

To end this section on Shrove Tuesday customs in Pennsylvania, I wish to share this "Fastnacht Song" recorded in the 1940s by Albert F. Buffington, Walter E. Boyer, and myself and published in our book, *Songs along the Mahantongo* (1951). It comes from the Mahantongo culture area in Schuylkill and Northumberland counties, north of Harrisburg. A delightful old woman in her nineties, Mary Ochs Paul, a native of the Mahantongo Valley, sang it for us. It is obviously a courting song that was once popular among the lusty, hot-blooded Mahantongo youth.

Siss net alli Daag luschdich Leewe,
Siss net alli Daag Faasenacht!
Ich hab mei Geld em Schpielmann gewwe
Un hab gedanst die ganse Nacht.

Dart drausse schteht en scheener Bu;
Wau er iss, des wees ich net.
Ich will geh en karressiere;
Maag mich liewe noch aach nicht.

Ach Buweli, ich hab Gold un Silwer!
Buweli, ich hab Haus un Lott!
Buweli, ich hab alli Gieder,
Was mann sich erwinschen kann.

Auwer liewer das ich mei yung frisch Leewe,
Soo me alde Wittmann geewe,
Liewer wollt ich Kuggele giesse
Fer denn alde Wittmann schiesse.

Mary Paul's song can be translated as follows:

> Every day you can't go a-sporting,
> Fastnacht is not every day.
> The fiddler took my cash for playing
> While I danced the night away.
>
> Out there stands such a handsome boy
> Who he is, alas, I don't know
> Yet will I go and give love's joy
> E'en though he answers "yes" or "no."
>
> Little boy, I have gold and silver,
> Little boy, I have house and lot.
> And little boy, I am no miser
> With all the riches I have got.
>
> Rather than give my fresh, young life
> To that widower, that old sot,
> Would I bullets be a-moulding
> To shoot him with a single shot!

Dr. Shoemaker mentions this song without quoting it (see page 6). He gives instead the first verse of another version recorded from the Hamburg area in Berks County. That one ends with "dreamed all night long" rather than "danced the night away" as in Mary Paul's version, but hers is probably closer to tradition. Dancing at the Fastnacht frolics and on many other occasions throughout the year was popular among most Pennsylvania Dutch groups, especially among those church groups (Lutheran and Reformed) that said "yes" to the world. And Mahantongo was one of the most lively centers for dancing and reveling on traditional holidays.

EASTER CUSTOMS IN EUROPEAN FOLK-CULTURE

The most concise reporting of Easter customs in Europe is Robert Wildhaber's symposium, "*Osterbrauchtum in Europa*" ("Easter Customs in Europe"), which took up an entire double issue in 1957 of the folk-cultural journal he edited for so many years, the *Schweizerisches Archiv für Volkskunde*. This collection of articles by leading European scholars covers Eastertide as celebrated in Switzerland, Germany (many areas), Austria, France (Alsace), Belgium, Holland, Norway, Finland, Estonia, Italy, Portugal, Slovenia (Yugoslavia), Czechoslovakia (Moravia, Slovakia), Poland, Hungary, Romania, Bulgaria, and Greece. The majority of the contributions deal with Easter eggs, their history, function, and decorations. Several deal with Easter foods, particularly Easter breads and other baked goods. Others treat the use of Easter eggs in folk medicine, and the egg in European folk riddles.

From the symposium we learn that in earlier centuries Easter eggs were much more a part of the formal culture than they are in America today, where individual families determine the range of the custom. Easter eggs used to be paid, for example, as part of one's tithe to the landlord, or given as festive (and expected!) gifts to the village pastor, the schoolmaster, the sexton and bellringer, the parish grave digger, and even the village shepherd. And of course they were hospitably presented to visitors, bestowed upon servants, and above all given to children. Courting couples exchanged them as tokens of love. And godparents usually regaled their godchildren with gifts of decorated eggs.

Editor Wildhaber himself contributed a major essay on the Easter rabbit and other Eastertide egg bringers. Like the Christmas tree, the Easter rabbit (actually the Easter hare in Europe) is not documented before the seventeenth century. The earliest documentation found thus far dates from 1682, when a Heidelberg doctor named Georg Frank published a book with the title *De ovis paschalibus— Von Oster-Eyern, Satyrae medicae* (*Of Easter Eggs, Satires of a Physician*). Although the Easter rabbit is the major egg supplier in German-speaking lands, there were runners-up in the form of "egg birds,"

An engraving from Switzerland of an Osterhase *with his basket of Easter eggs. Below, the children are arranging eggs for an Easter game. From* National-Kinderlieder für die Zürchersche Jugend *(Zurich, 1789).*

"Easter hens," cranes, storks, even foxes and other creatures. The Easter rabbit is a relatively recent arrival, and scholars are still debating the reasons for his presence in Easter custom and lore. It is generally thought that, like the Christmas tree, the custom of the *Osterhase* began in cities and filtered down into country villages from there. Among the theories of the Easter rabbit's origin, the most plausible (although still not without difficulties) is that it developed in the realm of Easter baked goods, when an earlier Easter cake in the shape of the Paschal lamb "misfired" and turned into a Paschal rabbit! Once established, the Easter rabbit was believed to actually lay the eggs. Hence children went to elaborate lengths to build attractive nests for the elusive egg producer, who was summoned by whistling or saying a charm.

If "Easter rabbit" seems an inexact translation of *Osterhase*, there is a logical explanation. The High German word *Osterhase* technically means "Easter hare." The German word for rabbit is *Kaninchen*, which is cognate with the English word *coney*, as in Coney Island. When our emigrant ancestors settled in Pennsylvania, they found no hares, but plenty of rabbits, hence we translate the Pennsylvania Dutch word *Oschterhaas* "Easter rabbit."

Printed imagery on the *Osterhase* is meager, but we include among the illustrations a charming frontispiece of a children's song book published in Zurich in 1789, showing at top center a vignette of an Easter rabbit and basket of eggs, and in the foreground children arranging eggs for an Easter game.

One of the many revelations in the Wildhaber symposium is that our Pennsylvania Dutch method of decorating Easter eggs with the pith of a rush plant (called in local dialect *Binsagraws*) is reported from the Odenwald area of southern Hessen, a region that produced much eighteenth-century emigration to Pennsylvania. This type of egg decoration is described in the article by Friedrich Mössinger entitled "Odenwälder Binseeier."

Because of their unusually designed decoration, such eggs are favorite holiday gifts to friends and family in the Odenwald. The eggs are not eaten, but rather are hung up for display, so the first step in their preparation is blowing out the contents of the shells. Chicken eggs are normally used, but sometimes larger duck and goose eggs are also decorated in this way. The marrow or pith of the *Binsen* (rushes) is easy to remove from the green stems in the springtime. The pith is looped around the eggs or applied in patterns (circles, spirals, crosses, hearts, etc.) and attached to the surface of the shell with flour paste. Some eggs are completely covered with the pith; others show the white shell through the applied designs. Sometimes colorful pieces of cloth are added to the decoration.

Some of the pith may also be colored—red, green, yellow—to elaborate the designs. For further amusement, three dried peas or pieces of hard sugar are inserted into the shell so that the egg rattles when shaken. And instead of being displayed in nests or Easter baskets, these unusual eggs are kept all year, suspended, usually three in a row, from the rafters of the farmhouse stove room (*Stube*) or hanging from the ceiling lamps. In Catholic homes they are often placed on the holy corner shelf above the dining table, in the belief that they bring the household happiness and blessing.

Because of the obvious fragility of egg shells, the evidence of such eggs in the Odenwald has been traced back only into the nineteenth century, through interviews with persons born before 1900. They are very probably older, since they are found in other Hessian areas, in Saxony, and even farther

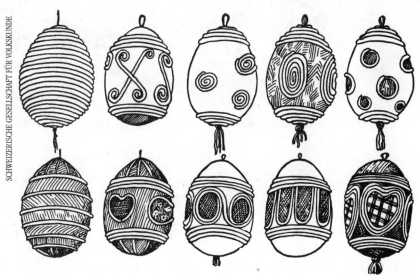

SCHWEIZERISCHE GESELLSCHAFT FÜR VOLKSKUNDE

Binsa-graws *Easter egg decoration as practised in the Odenwald area of Hessen. The patterns shown here from different villages in the region are similar to those used in Pennsylvania. Top row from left: Aschbach, Würzberg, Würzberg, Hüttenthal, Aschbach (?). Bottom row from left: Museum Darmstadt, Museum Darmstadt, Pfirschbach, Kimbach, Mossau. From the* Schweizerisches Archiv für Volkskunde *(1957).*

Patricia Wynnysky, of Bethlehem, Pennsylvania, and daughter decorating Easter eggs in the Ukrainian tradition.

afield, in the Lausitz, and in the Egerland in the former Czechoslovakia.

The same article by Mössinger offers another surprising link to Pennsylvania Dutch Easter customs. In the Odenwald some of these pith-decorated Easter eggs were used to make *Ostervögel* (Easter birds). These were made of goose eggs and hung up horizontally, as if flying through the air with their diminutive paper wings (see page 29).

Of British books on Easter, Venetia Newall's *An Egg at Easter: A Folklore Study* (1971) is the most expert introduction in English to the history of the

Easter egg and its place in ecclesiastical and folk culture. The book discusses the egg in general as a symbol of creation; its use in primitive sacrifice, witchcraft, and magic; and its connection with fertility, purity, and resurrection. The data reflect the comparative folklore approach used by early folklorists in Britain. Evidence is cited from many primitive and Christian cultures the world over, but with concentration on Europe and America.

The sections on egg decoration are thorough and include the significance of the color red (for magic, renewal of life, Christ's blood, and resurrection). All forms of decoration (coloring, scratching, etching, and appliqué) are discussed, with many pertinent illustrations, many in striking full color. Art eggs of porcelain, glass, and other materials are included as well.

Chapters on the egg tree and Easter pastimes and games conclude the book, which has a nineteen-page bibliography. And we are pleased to report that Dr. Newall cites *Eastertide in Pennsylvania* several times and includes several illustrations from the book, among them our prize Pennsylvania Dutch egg-laying rabbit cake!

EASTER EGG DECORATION IN OTHER PENNSYLVANIA ETHNIC CULTURES

When we renamed our periodical *Pennsylvania Folklife* in 1958, both Alfred Shoemaker and I hoped to make it a clearinghouse for articles on the cultures of all the ethnic groups that make Pennsylvania such a fascinating multicultural phenomenon. It was our hope to include not only the folk cultures of the past, those of the Quakers, Scotch-Irish, and Pennsylvania Dutch, but also those of the present, from the nineteenth- and twentieth-century migrations across the Atlantic. We looked forward to including work done by recent scholars on American Indian, African-American, Hispanic-American, and Asian-American groups in Pennsylvania, examining their historic and present-day cultural status.

It was an ambitious program, but, as it turned out, the bulk of the research that landed on the editors' desks concerned the Pennsylvania Dutch. When I succeeded Alfred Shoemaker as editor in 1961, however, I corralled for the journal significant graduate term papers written for my University of Pennsylvania folklife studies courses. These included treatments of various aspects of Italian-American, Greek-American, and African-American cultures. Then in 1972 I published a pioneering article entitled "The Ukrainian Pysanka and Other

Decorated Easter Eggs in Pennsylvania," by Dr. Wasyl O. Luciw and George Wynnysky. (The term *pysanka*, plural *pysanky*, means "Easter egg.")

As background, Ukrainian emigration to Pennsylvania began in the late nineteenth century, with large numbers settling alongside Russians, Poles, and other eastern Europeans in the anthracite coal-mining regions of Eastern Pennsylvania and the bituminous mining areas of Western Pennsylvania. Russian and Ukrainian Orthodox Christians brought their colorful wooden church architecture with the golden domes and icon screens, their round of church holidays, their thrilling choral singing at Christmas and Easter, and their unusual methods of decorating Easter eggs.

Easter egg decoration in eastern Europe is an ancient folk art treasured in families and passed down from generation to generation. In their article, Luciw and Wynnysky describe a variety of motifs—geometrical, animal, and floral designs. The geometrical motifs are probably the oldest and range from "simple horizontal and vertical lines to section the egg, to sun symbols like the tripod, to the different 'endless line' forms, to the most complex 'star' or 'rosette' patterns." Animal and bird designs are rarest of all, but the reindeer is said to symbolize "wealth and prosperity," while a hen, or the feet of a hen, "symbolizes fertility and fulfillment of wishes." Butterflies, fish, and horses are also occasionally included in the design repertoire. From the plant world, pine trees are drawn to symbolize "eternal youth and health." In addition, apples are sometimes portrayed and, among floral designs, the periwinkle.

The article was based in part on interviews with Ukrainian-American egg decorators in several Ukrainian settlements of Pennsylvania. Many of the methods of decoration (dyeing, painting, scratching, waxing, etc.) are similar to Pennsylvania Dutch methods, but the range of motifs is somewhat different and the final products are often

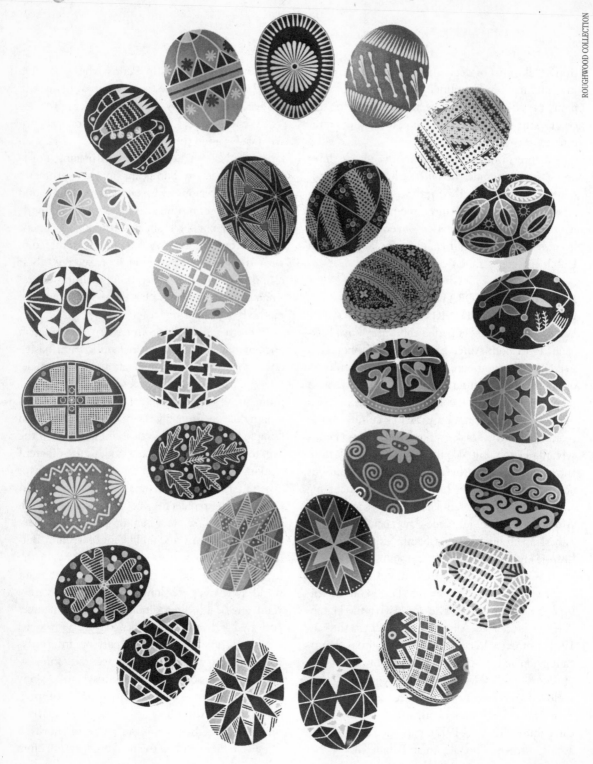

spectacular. Background colors are usually red or black, but also yellow and green. And many decorated eggs are multicolored. The illustrations we include are interesting to compare with the scratch-carved eggs pictured with Dr. Shoemaker's original text.

RECENT RESEARCH ON HOLIDAYS IN AMERICAN SCHOLARSHIP

The spring holidays, as well as all American holidays and their folk and pop-cultural customs, are examined in Jack Santino's *All Around the Year: Holidays and Celebrations in American Life* (1994), a useful and attractively written source.

Santino introduces the subject with an analysis of various theories on ritual, festival, and celebration, but the major part of the work deals with seasonal calendric holidays. Chapters include "Winter into Spring: Celebrating Birth and Renewal"; "Toward Midsummer: Celebrating the Season of the Sun"; and "Autumn into Winter: Celebrating Death and Life."

The book is ecumenical in its scope. One chapter discusses Valentine's Day, St. Patrick's Day, Carnival, Mardi Gras, Tet, All Fools Day, Passover, and Easter. The midsummer chapter continues with May Day, Whitsun, Memorial Day, Flag Day, Independence Day, and Labor Day.

Insightful on meanings and functions of all these holidays as celebrated by the American people, it is also a delight to read. The author, whom I am happy to name as a former student of mine, has cast it in an attractive personalized vein, sharing with the reader his own childhood memories of holiday participation and celebration.

Samples of original designs for Easter eggs in Pennsylvania's Ukrainian enclaves.

A PLEA FOR FESTIVITY AND FANTASY

Having briefly discussed European and American research on Fastnacht and Easter customs and their relation to the holiday customs preserved in Pennsylvania, let us turn in conclusion to an exciting American examination of the meaning of the festival phenomenon in human culture.

Among the most penetrating treatments by American scholars on the value of holiday celebration is *The Feast of Fools: A Theological Essay on Festivity and Fantasy* (1970). The author, Harvey Cox, of Harvard Divinity School, is a native of Malvern, Pennsylvania, of Baptist and Quaker family background (two Pennsylvania groups that ironically were earlier opposed to festivities and even to Christmas and Easter). The book laments the loss of the celebratory aspects of human life since the Middle Ages. The blame, according to Cox, rests partly on Protestantism, the Reformation having laid heavy stress upon man's daily work and duty, leaving little time for festivity. The Industrial Revolution and modern capitalism further emphasized the virtues of "sobriety, thrift, industry, and ambition" and increased the stress on daily work by removing it from the home to the factory and office. Additional factors in downgrading festivity and fantasy in human life have been modern science, secularism, and religious and cultural pluralism. As Professor Cox puts it:

Celebration requires a set of common memories and collective hopes. It requires, in short, what is usually thought of as a religion. For centuries Christianity provided our civilization with both the feast days that kept its history alive, and with the images of the future that sustained its expectations. Stories of Adam, Noah, and Abraham rooted us in the recesses of our prehistory. The saints supplied images of human perfection. The Kingdom of God and the New Jerusalem with their visions of peace and social fulfillment kept us hopeful about the future. At Christmas and Easter, and to some extent during the other

In 1801. march 4. the administration of Thomas Jefferson commenced in york the bury the Black Cockade. riband worn on the hat. democratical by George Spangler. Fred Rockey. Conrad Welshans. Henry weiser Salmon Mues. michael Edward. at furry's tavern. John Stued. John Stroman. John weyer.

Mr Barnhard. A vender give to little Lewis Miller. the first Barlo-Knife as A present. 1799.

Yearly Market, or publick fare.

Held in the Borough of York, June 9th 1801. the had privilege of a Stated yearly market.

In 1816. the prohibited the holding of fairs within the Borough of York. and declared Such holding a common nuisance. in Some dispute at Lewis Wampler. tavern — michael Hahn. Stop — Robert Dunn; and at the Same time — nickolas Scheffer cut Barnhard with a Knife. at Eberhart. tavern.

holy days, the figure of Jesus somehow enlivened both our primal memories and our wildest hopes. The last of the prophets of Israel, Jesus was also seen as the first citizen of an epoch still to be fulfilled. Thus did Western man, richly supplied with cultural memories and vivid aspirations, once celebrate his place in history and in the cosmos.

In earlier folk societies, especially in the peasant villages of Europe from which our Pennsylvania Dutch families derived most of their traditions, there was a wholesome alternation between work and worship, and an equally wholesome alternation between work and leisure. The festival calendar of the medieval church, taken over in part by Protestantism, provided our ancestors with many days and seasons when hard daily work could be shelved for a time and man could give way to festivity, celebration, fantasy, and play.

In analyzing a festive occasion, Cox points to three essential ingredients: conscious excess, celebrative affirmation, and juxtaposition. Conscious excess means festive activity that is intentionally overdone. By celebrative affirmation Cox suggests that in the festival—freed for a time from our daily round of work—we "say yes to life." Juxtaposition "means that festivity must display contrast" to make it obviously different from "everyday life." Our Pennsylvania Dutch spring festivals, several of which involved revelry, dressing in special garb

A drawing of the festivities at the annual York Fair in June 1801 by Lewis Miller (1796–1882). Note the performers in the foreground with their eager audience of children. Booths for food and merchant goods were erected near the court house, and the market shed was also used. This picture gives us a magnificent glimpse into the sense of festivity and enjoyment of life that reigned in the Pennsylvania Dutch Country at holiday time.

(including cross-dressing), dancing, feasting, and drinking, meet all three of Cox's requirements.

Festivals also give us a sense of sacred time, which relates past, present, and future to human life. And the "common memories and collective hopes" that were necessary for celebration were all present in the earlier folk societies of our European ancestors. Alas, they are largely missing from our present-day pluralistic society, where every individual belongs not to one central, traditional group (village community and village church) but to many different and in some cases conflicting organizations.

Cox's book is full of insights on man's need for festivity and fantasy, and sounds a call to reconsider the way in which our society has moved away from both. He expresses all this, finally, in the statement: "Man is essentially festive and fanciful. To become fully human, Western industrial man, and his non-Western brothers insofar as they are touched by the same debilitation, must learn again to dance and to dream."

Alfred Shoemaker would have applauded Professor Cox's plea for festivity and fantasy. I always sensed that under the professorial and ministerial manner, with its scholarly pronouncements, there was a joyous human being who basically approved of the festive elements of our historic Pennsylvania Dutch culture and their roots in European cultures across the Atlantic. In the many years that I worked closely with him on all our many joint projects, I could not help but recognize the basic humanness and humane dimensions of his personality. My hope is that this reissue and expansion of his pioneering book on our springtime festivals will continue to remind the Pennsylvania Dutch people of Alfred Shoemaker's contributions to their own sense of identity in relation to the overarching culture of America.

Don Yoder
Fastnacht 2000

Notes

SHROVE TUESDAY

1. Clayton L. Keener, of Refton, Lancaster County, tells me in his family the last person out of bed on Shrove Tuesday is nicknamed *der sei-kivvel* (the swill-bucket). The Reverend A. C. Wuchter wrote a dialect poem in which he says the one who will be the fastnacht will be put in the swill-barrel (*Pennsylvania German,* April 1902, pages 61–63):

> *Ich wunner wer die Fahsnacht gebt?*
> *Wen's drefft der wert in's seifoss g'schperrt.*

MAUNDY THURSDAY

1. Hay was similarly put out in the barnyard on Christmas Eve and then fed to the farm animals on Christmas morning. For a discussion of this practice, see my book *Christmas in Pennsylvania.*

EASTER LORE

1. Like nature, the human likes to put on a completely new garb at this time of year. The Mauch Chunk *Gazette* of April 7, 1853—just over a century ago—put it this way:

An old time conceit, that one must have some part of his clothes new on Easter day, has not yet disappeared; we can well remember the new hat, shoes or gloves, with which, in our youth we were decked on that day.

> At Easter let your clothes be new,
> Or else be sure you will it rue.

The only bit of folklore regarding new clothes for Easter that I have ever collected in the Dutch Country I have from Mrs. Paul Werly, of Weisenberg Township, Lehigh County: *Wammer en nei-i pawr shtrimp aw-dutt uff die Oschdera, dann watt mer seilaives net grank.* (If one puts on a new pair of stockings on Easter one will not become ill ever.)

2. Another bit of information Mr. Smith was able to add to our knowledge of early customs in the Dutch Country is the existence of small cardboard boxes made by the early tramp craftsmen and used to hold an individual presentation Easter egg. Mr. Smith, a close student of old days, has mastered the making of these Easter egg boxes and has produced a small number for his own use.

3. The major part of Dr. Witmer's article follows:

A few years ago there passed away in our city one of the most noted creators of mechanical ideas in America. He had invented, improved, changed and devised so many mechanical contrivances, he actually had over a thousand patents granted by the United States government, up until that time an unheard of record.

To tabulate his numerous inventions would require more space than is allotted to this department. Happily most of his patents were for worthwhile improvements. Things of practical, everyday nature, the production of which brought about the employment of numerous men and requiring several acres of machinery. Some of his ideas were so practical they, upon being manufactured, became a portion of an international business which sprang up through their sales so that today many of them are distributed throughout the civilized world, no suitable substitute having been found to take the place of these inventions.

The field of mechanical invention, like that of literary production, is not confined to one person or a single group of people, nor a single line of invention; it is broad and wide. Patents are procurable upon every conceivable device or idea under the canopy of heaven. What is required in the patent department is that the idea cover something new, something never before patented or a decided improvement on something already patented. Each application for a patent is scrutinized closely to determine its originality or to detect any infringement upon a patent already granted or issued. Though all manner of word pictures have been produced by our Lancaster literary people and in spite of the fact that so many mechanical contrivances have been offered the public, once more it is a pleasure to record the invention some years ago of an entirely new idea, one in a fruitful field but one entirely unexploited. Like other inventions it is so simple and interesting one cannot but wonder it had not been worked out long years earlier.

Candy Models

About Easter time one sees in the shop windows, among vendors on the streets and in confectionery stores, oddly shaped candy pigs, peculiar looking rabbits, Easter eggs; in fact numerous fantastic candy models, novelties usually coated with chocolate and bedecked with vari-colored lines and curves of candy ornamentation. The method of making these curious specimens of a semi-artistic nature was devised by a Lancaster man years ago. They became so popular and grew to be such an important part of Lancaster's many sided productions that they attracted the attention of manufacturers and producers out of our city who came here to learn how these interesting novelties were made. They acquired the knack quietly and quickly, then went back home and turned out thousands of these interesting Easter novelties. Others learned, only to pass it on to still newer aspirants until the methods became spread throughout the length and breadth of the land, later spreading into several foreign countries where they have proven equally as popular as in the U. S. A.

Method of Making

The method of producing these interesting confections is interesting and while requiring a considerable amount of artistic skill, is not difficult or long drawn out. The first move is to make a model delineating the pose, every curve, groove and line exactly as it is wanted in the finished product. It is imperative that each little part shall be absolutely accurate and correct, for any defect or defection in the original model or sample will be reproduced in the finished article. In other words the finished confections are simply replicas of the original model, hence it becomes evident that any distortion of the model will be reproduced much to the detriment of the finished object.

Original Pattern

The original pattern or model is made of paraffin, wax or some similar substance which is first modeled as near to the finished form as possible. The details are carved and carefully finished to suit the particular fancy of the manufacturer. This carving must be done when the paraffin is cold and stiff, otherwise the various grooves and lines will [not] be sharp and clearly defined, causing a dull, uninteresting model and likewise finished article.

When the model or pattern is constructed and finished as required, it is oiled all over. Plaster of Paris is mixed very thin and poured into a container or box considerably larger than the model.

The model is now placed in the plaster exactly in the center so that a liberal margin of plaster surrounds the model, one half being immersed, the other portion extending above the level of the plaster. The surface of edge extending around the partly submerged model is smoothed off and oiled very carefully; sometimes it is varnished to prevent sticking. The unsubmerged portion of the model extends up in relief. It is now covered over with a second "mix" of plaster which entirely submerges the model and also extends the first "pour" of plaster. When the whole mass has become hard (that is, has set) the outer container is taken off and the two halves of the plaster cast are separated at the oiled division. The paraffin is heated and made soft and entirely removed leaving a hollow—a negative—the exact replica of the paraffin model. Small vents are cut between the two parts to permit pouring the molten candy. The two parts are replaced, fitting exactly and fastened together. The operator at this point has a sizable block of hard plaster with a hollow center, a small vent to the outside to the hollow. The proposed candy or cream is melted and gently poured into the hollow opening, the whole cast being agitated to permit air bubbles to escape. When filled the form and contents are placed in the cold until the candy becomes crystallized or hard. The two parts are separated and the candy replica is lifted out, an exact reproduction of the original model so carefully shaped.

Reproduced in Candy

It is most interesting to note how accurately the wax pattern is reproduced in candy. The next move is to dress up the candy model. This is usually done with melted chocolate being poured over or daubed on in spots. When coated as desired, the ornamental lines are placed, also eyes or any decorative feature desired. The original idea was evolved from the fertile brains of Joseph Huber and Joe Royer, two master confectioners of a generation ago. They were great cronies and business associates who worked together. The first Easter toys and candy specialties were made by them and offered for sale in Royers' Confectionery Store on West King street and at Anderson's on East King street next to the Farmers Trust Co. When the plan of making Easter specialties was first talked of among dealers, the originators of this idea were laughed out of the meeting; it was considered too ridiculous for words to think that anyone would attempt a special effort on Easter novelties particularly rabbits, pigs and candy eggs. However time vindicated their judgment, and today Easter specialties are a real feature of the business.

The first models used to produce the forms were clear toys. Forms were made from these candies and later cast in cream to be coated and ornamented with chocolate or whatever [the] fancy or the whims of the trade may require. As time passed certain innovations and refinements have been introduced. So that today glossy neat confections are turned out of metal casts, the natural outgrowth of plaster forms. These smooth, almost burnished products are very attractive and have a strong appeal. This invention like many others only required someone to show the way (break the trail), others soon followed. The idea recommended itself. It was grasped by others who put it to good use. Many modifications and innovations have been introduced with the result that today thousands of varieties of confections are for sale, many of which were produced by some modification of this method, most of which are a joy and delight to the young ones.

Easter with its spring atmosphere, its flowers and bright colors, its beautifully dyed eggs and marvelous rabbits, has grown yearly until it has developed into as lavish a celebration as Christmas. In any event the day is well worth celebrating, it assuredly gives the kiddies a day long thrill. Happy indeed is Lancaster to have contributed so largely to the immense enjoyment of this day.

Hollow Candy Toys

Another variety of toy confection which appeals to the youthful mind is the chocolate specimens produced at this season of the year which are hollow. They are made up in a number of shapes and sizes and are a source of curiosity to many purchasers because of being simply a shell of chocolate, some with a thin base, others open at the lower part or base. These too are an outgrowth of the Huber invention. The form in which they are cast is made of white metal finished with great accuracy, the form is in two parts. These two sections are oiled and placed together, being fastened tightly. Chocolate of the required kind is fused in a metal container, this is poured in the hollow model form.

The outer surface of chocolate or the part in contact with the metal becomes cooled and gets hard. If permitted to remain the whole mass would become rigid but as soon as the outer edge or shell grows stiff and hard the form is turned upside down and the center or soft chocolate flows out, leaving the shell remaining in the form. This is now thoroughly chilled, the parts of the form separated and out drops the hollow toy. When a base is required a layer of molten chocolate is poured on a pan or smooth metal which has been oiled. When this layer is soft the hollow toy is placed upon its base down. As it becomes cold the thin layer adheres to the toy and is removed from the pan or metal. The edge is trimmed to conform with the outlines or lower portion of the toy. In this way a hollow toy is made and sealed up completely at the base.

Originality in any shape is a valuable asset. In an invention of this type it is doubly desirable because it creates a means for numerous people to gain a living. It is possible to broaden the field of its usefulness creating many variations, all of which are a source of profit to manufacturers and a great source of joy to the final purchasers. The celebration of Easter has grown immensely within the last generation. Especially so among confectioners and hot houses. Indeed the display of flowers at Easter or just before has grown to be an event of great importance in our city. Thousands of dollars worth are raised and coerced to bloom just in time for the Easter celebration. Of all decorative features at this season none appear so appropriate and so well timed as beautiful flowers. Let us hope this custom will develop and broaden as years go by.

THE EASTER RABBIT

1. There is reference to the growing popularity of the Easter rabbit in *Christian Culture* for April 1, 1891, which quotes an article by Katharine Hillard in the *Atlantic Monthly*:

For more seasons than one cares to count, the Easter egg has been the familiar symbol of the great spring festival; but of late years, owing probably to the immense increase of our foreign population, another emblem has begun to dispute its supremacy in the confectioners' shops and for some time the hares at Easter have been almost as numerous as the eggs.

ASCENSION DAY

1. A folk belief collected from Mrs. Weda Wolfinger of Kutztown, January 11, 1957: "An oldtime belief was that if one used a pair of scissors on Ascension Day snakes would invade the house during the coming months."

2. Edwin M. Fogel has this folk belief in his *Beliefs and Superstitions of the Pennsylvania Germans* (page 124): "Many women will die in confinement if there are thunderstorms on Ascension Day."

3. Dialect columnist Dr. Pierce Swope wrote a Pennsylvania Dutch poem, entitled "*Fische Geh*" (Going Fishing) on May 18, 1950, for Ascension Day. It was published in Dr. Arthur D. Graeff's "*Scholla*" column in the Reading *Times* on May 21, 1952.

WHITSUNTIDE

1. The number seven derives, of course, from the fact that Whitsunday is the seventh Sunday after Easter. Two sources indicate a number of rainy Sundays other than seven. James L. Morris, a storekeeper of Morgantown, Berks County, entered in his diary on May 29, 1842 (manuscript at the Berks County Historical Society): "According to some of the Germans we are still to have five more wet Sabbaths because Whit Sunday was wet." And John Bear Stoudt, in an article "Weather-Prognostications and Superstitions among the Pennsylvania Germans" (*Pennsylvania German*, volume 7, page 243), recorded: "Rain on Whitsunday will be followed by six rainy Sundays."

2. Reformed clergymen early raised objection to a special garb at confirmation, e.g., the *Messenger* of April 1833, pages 25–26:

Confirmation. We dislike the practice of having the catecumens to recite, what they have learned, in the presence of the congregation: still less do we approve the expensive and useless pomp of a peculiar dress for the occasion.

3. An informant, Jacob Bachman of the Eck, Berks County, told the author a number of years ago that a child who attended catechetical instruction was called a *parres-kind* (minister's child). He said parents were very strict with such children. He added: "Why children attending catechetical instruction used not to be allowed event to attend public sales, so strict the old folks were in this matter."

4. Mrs. Reeser's recipe for egg cheese: six quarts of sweet milk, one quart buttermilk, twelve eggs. Heat sweet milk almost to boiling point; add beaten eggs and buttermilk; leave on back of stove until it forms chunks and then put in a cloth to drain; serve the following day.

Further Reading

Arnott, Margaret. "Easter Eggs and Easter Bread of South-eastern Pennsylvania." *Expedition* 3, no. 3 (spring 1961): 24–33.

Bächtold-Stäubli, Hanns, and Eduard Hoffmann-Krayer, eds. *Handwörterbuch des Deutschen Aberglaubens.* 2d ed. 10 vols. Berlin: Walter de Gruyter, 1987.

Barba, Preston A. *Pennsylvania German Tombstones: A Study in Folk Art.* Allentown, Pa.: Schlechter's, 1954. *The Pennsylvania German Folklore Society* 18 (1953).

Bardout, Michèle. *La Paille et le Feu: Traditions vivantes d'Alsace.* Paris: Berger-Levrault, 1980.

Barrick, Mac E. *German-American Folklore.* Little Rock, Ark.: August House, 1987.

Bausinger, Hermann. *Volkskunde in der technischen Welt.* Stuttgart: W. Kohlhammer, 1961.

Becker, Albert. *Osterei und Osterhase: vom Brauchtum der deutschen Osterzeit.* Jena: E. Diederichs, 1937.

———. *Pfälzer Frühlingsfeiern: Beiträge zur Heimatkunde der Pfalz* 10. Kaiserslautern, 1908.

Bede, The Venerable. *The Ecclesiastical History of the English Nation.* London: J. M. Dent, 1910.

Benz, Ernst. "On Understanding Non-Christian Religions." In: *The History of Religions: Essays in Methodology,* edited by Mircea Eliade and Joseph Kitagawa, 115–131. Chicago: University of Chicago Press, 1959.

Best, Martha S. "Easter Customs in the Lehigh Valley." *Pennsylvania Folklife* 17, no. 3 (spring 1968): 2–13.

Bradshaw, Paul F., and Lawrence A. Hoffman, eds. *Passover and Easter: Origin and History in Modern Times.* Notre Dame, Ind.: University of Notre Dame Press, 1999.

———. *Passover and Easter: The Symbolic Structuring of Sacred Seasons.* Notre Dame, Ind.: University of Notre Dame Press, 1999.

Brand, John. *Observations on Popular Antiquities.* New Castle upon Tyne: J. Johnson, 1777.

Brednich, Rolf W., ed. *Grundrisse der Volkskunde: Einführung in die Forschungsfelder der Europäischen Ethnologie.* 2d ed., rev. and enl. Berlin: Dietrich Reimer Verlag, 1994. See especially Andreas C. Bimmer, "Brauchforschung," pages 375–395, with extensive bibliography.

Brewer, E. Cobham. *Dictionary of Phrase and Fable.* 6th ed. Philadelphia: Claxton, Remsen, and Haffelfinger, n.d.

Bronner, Simon J. *Following Tradition: Folklore in the Discourse of American Culture.* Logan, Utah: Utah State University Press, 1998. See chapter 6, "Alfred Shoemaker and the Discovery of American Folklife," pages 266–312.

———. "A Prophetic Vision: Alfred Shoemaker and America's First Department of Folklore." *Folklore Historian* 8 (1991): 38–55.

———. "Shoemaker vs. Shoemaker: The Debate on Pennsylvania Germans in American Tradition." *Der Reggeboge/The Rainbow: Journal of the Pennsylvania German Society* 30, nos. 1–2 (1996): 3–30.

Brunner, Frank R. "Ostere." In: *Pennsylvania German: A Collection of Pennsylvania German Productions in Poetry and Prose,* 2d ed. Edited by Daniel Miller, 74–78. Reading, Pa.: Daniel Miller, 1904.

Brunvand, Jan Harold, ed. *American Folklore: An Encyclopedia.* New York: Garland, 1996.

Caplow, Theodore, and Margaret Holmes Williamson. "Decoding Middletown's Easter Bunny: A Study in American Iconography." *Semiotica* 32 (1980): 221–232.

Christ, Robert B., and Eugen A. Meier. *Fasnacht in Basel.* Basel: Pharos-Verlag, 1968.

Clements, William M. "Easter." In: *American Folklore: An Encyclopedia,* edited by Jan Harold Brunvand, 217–218. New York: Garland, 1996.

Cohen, Hennig, and Tristram Potter Coffin, eds. *The Folklore of American Holidays.* 2d ed. Detroit: Gale, 1991.

Cox, Harvey. *The Feast of Fools: A Theological Essay on Festivity and Fantasy.* New York: Harper and Row, 1970.

Dörfliche Fasnacht zwischen Neckar und Bodensee: Beiträge des Tübinger Arbeitskreises für Fasnachtsforschung. Tübingen: Tübinger Vereinigung für Volkskunde, 1966.

Dörrer, Anton. *Tiroler Fasnacht, innerhalb der alpenländischen Winter- und Vorfrühlingsbraüche.* Vienna: Österreichischer Bundesverlag für Unterricht, Wissenschaft und Kunst, 1949.

Dorson, Richard M., ed. *Folklore and Folklife: An Introduction.* Chicago: University of Chicago Press, 1972. For a good overall view of the history of the subject, weighted toward folklore but including folklife, see the editor's introduction, "Concepts of Folklore and Folklife Studies," pages 1–50.

———, ed. *Peasant Customs and Savage Myths: Selections from the British Folklorists.* 2 vols. London: Routledge and Kegan Paul, 1968.

Erich, Oswald A., and Richard Beitl. *Wörterbuch der Deutschen Volkskunde.* 3d ed. Edited by Richard Beitl and Klaus Beitl. Stuttgart: Alfred Kröner Verlag, 1974. See articles *"Fasnacht," "Aschermittwoch," "Gründonnerstag," "Karfreitag," "Ostern," "Himmelfahrt Christi,"* and *"Pfingst(en)."*

Fasnacht: Beiträge des Tübinger Arbeitskreises für Fasnachtsforschung. Tübingen: Tübinger Vereinigung für Volkskunde, 1964.

"Fastnacht." In: *Handwörterbuch des Deutschen Aberglaubens,* vol. 2, cols. 1246–1261. 2d ed. Berlin: Walter de Gruyter, 1987.

Fehrle, Eugen. *Deutsche Feste und Volksbräuche.* Leipzig: B. G. Teubner, 1920.

———. *Feste und Volksbräuche im Jahreslauf europäischer Völker.* Kassel: J. P. Hinnenthal, 1955.

Fogel, Edwin M. *Beliefs and Superstitions of the Pennsylvania Germans.* Philadelphia: Americana Germanica Press, 1915.

———. "Of Months and Days." *Pennsylvania German Folklore Society* 5 (1940): 1–23.

———. *Proverbs of the Pennsylvania Germans.* Lancaster, Pa.: Lancaster Press, 1929. *The Pennsylvania-German Society, Proceedings and Addresses* 36 (1929).

Franck, Georgius. *De ovis paschalibus—Von Oster-Eyern, satyrae medicae.* Heidelberg, 1682.

Frazer, James G. *The Golden Bough: A Study in Magic and Religion.* 12 vols. 3d. ed. London: Macmillan, 1911–1915.

Fryer, Judith E. *25 Year Index to* Pennsylvania Folklife *(including* The Pennsylvania Dutchman *and* The Dutchman*), Volumes 1–25, 1949–1976.* Collegeville, Pa: Pennsylvania Folklife Society, 1980. See pages 44–45 for articles on Easter and other spring festivals by Alfred L. Shoemaker. The index also includes all the student papers on customs of the year mentioned in Dr. Shoemaker's text.

Gaster, Theodore H. *Festivals of the Jewish Year: A Modern Interpretation and Guide.* New York: Sloane, 1963.

Gibbons, Phebe Earle. *"Pennsylvania Dutch," and Other Essays.* 3d ed. Philadelphia: J. B. Lippincott, 1882.

Gray, Nada. *Holidays: Victorian Women Celebrate in Pennsylvania.* University Park, Pa.: Pennsylvania State University Press, 1983.

Grimm, Jacob. *Teutonic Mythology.* 4 vols. Translated by James Steven Stallybrass. Reprint of the first London edition, 1883–1888. New York: Dover Publications, 1966.

Haug, Walter, and Rainer Warning, eds. *Das Fest.* Munich: Wilhelm Fink Verlag, 1989.

Henisch, Bridget Ann. *Fast and Feast: Food in Medieval Society.* University Park, Pa.: Pennsylvania State University Press, 1976.

Hepding, Hugo. "Ostereier und Osterhase." *Hessische Blätter für Volkskunde* 26 (1927): 127–141.

Hoffmann-Krayer, Eduard. *Feste und Bräuche des Schweizervolkes: Kleines Handbuch der schweizerischen Volksbräuche der Gegenwart in gemeinschaftlicher Darstellung.* Zurich: Schulthess, 1913.

Hole, Christina. *British Folk Customs.* London: Hutchinson & Co., 1976.

———. *Easter and Its Customs: A Brief Study.* London: R. Bell, 1961.

Horne, A. R. *Horne's Pennsylvania German Manual.* 3d ed. Allentown, Pa.: T. K. Horne, 1905.

Kălcik, Susan. "The Folk Art of Decorated Eggs." *Pennsylvania Folklife* 44, no. 3 (spring 1995): 118–125.

Keddigkeit, Jürgen, ed. *Feste und Festbräuche in der Pfalz.* Kaiserslautern: Institut für pfälzische Geschichte und Volkskunde, 1992.

Kelm, Antje, et al. *Ostereier: Vom Symbol des Lebens zum Konsumartikel.* Hamburg: Hamburgisches Museum für Völkerkunde, 1981.

Kieffer, Elizabeth Clarke. "Easter Customs of Lancaster County." *Papers Read before the Lancaster County Historical Society* 52, no. 3 (1948): 49–68.

Kohler, Erika. *Martin Luther und der Festbrauch*. Cologne: Böhlau Verlag, 1959.

Kramer, Dieter. *German Holidays and Folk Customs*. 7th ed. Bonn: Atlantik-Brücke, 1986.

Künzig, Johannes. *Die alemannisch-schwäbische Fasnet*. Freiburg im Breisgau: Landesstelle für Volkskunde, 1950.

Kurrus, Theodor. "Theologische Aspekte der Fastnacht." In: *Fasnacht*, 80–98. Tübingen: Tübinger Vereinigung für Volkskunde, 1964.

Küster, Jürgen. "Fastnachtsgebote als Quellen: Zur Interpretation archivalischer Zeugnisse." *Jahrbuch für Volkskunde* 6 (1983): 53–74.

"Langschläfer." *Hanwörterbuch des Deutschen Aberglaubens*, vol. 5, cols. 902–904. 2d ed. Berlin: Walter de Gruyter, 1987.

Lefftz, Joseph. *Elsässische Volksleben im Osterfrühling*. Strasbourg: Culture Alsacienne, 1974.

Lehmann, Hedi. *Volksbrauch im Jahreslauf*. Munich: Ernst Heimeran Verlag, 1964.

Lessa, William A., and Evon Z. Vogt, eds. *Reader in Comparative Religion: An Anthropological Approach*. 3d ed. New York: Harper and Row, 1972.

Lichten, Frances. *Folk Art of Rural Pennsylvania*. New York: Charles Scribner's Sons, 1946.

Luciw, Wasyl O., and George Wynnysky. "The Ukrainian Pysanka and Other Decorated Easter Eggs in Pennsylvania." *Pennsylvania Folklife* 21, no. 3 (spring 1972): 2–7.

Mannhardt, Wilhelm. *Wald- und Feldkulte*. 2 vols. Darmstadt: Wissenschaftliche Buchgesellschaft, 1963. Facsimile reprint of second edition (Berlin 1905).

Matter, Max, ed. "Rheinischer Karneval." *Rheinisches Jahrbuch für Volkskunde* 23 (Bonn, 1978).

McNeill, John Thomas. *Modern Christian Movements*. Philadelphia: Westminster Press, 1954. See chapters on Puritanism, Pietism, and Evangelicalism.

Milhous, Katherine. *The Egg Tree*. New York: Scribner, 1950.

Moser, Hans. "Osterei und Ostergebäck: Brauchgeschichtliches aus bayerischen Quellen." *Bayerisches Jahrbuch für Volkskunde* (1957): 67–89.

———. *Volksbräuche im geschichtlichen Wandel*. Munich: Deutscher Kunstverlag, 1985.

Newall, Venetia. *An Egg at Easter: A Folklore Study*. Bloomington, Ind.: Indiana University Press, 1971.

O'Sullivan, Sean. *A Handbook of Irish Folklore*. Dublin: The Educational Company of Ireland, Ltd., 1942.

Owen, Trefor M. *Welsh Folk Customs*. Cardiff: National Museum of Wales, Welsh Folk Museum, 1959.

Pessler, Wilhelm, ed. *Handbuch der Deutschen Volkskunde*. 3 vols. Potsdam: Akademische Verlagsgesellschaft Athenaion, 1934.

Program 6th Annual Pennsylvania Dutch Folk Festival, June 30 to July 4, 1955—Kutztown, Pa. Kutztown, Pa.: Pennsylvania Dutch Folk Festival, 1955. See especially "The Folklore Center," pages 24–27; "Staff of the Folklore Center," pages 28–31; "The Center's Genealogical Program," pages 32–33; and "The Dutchman," pages 34–35.

"Religion." In: *Handwörterbuch des Deutschen Aberglaubens*. 2d ed. Vol. 7, cols. 652–681. Berlin: Walter de Gruyter, 1987.

Rodrigue, Denise. *Cycle de Pâques au Québec et dans l'Ouest de la France*. Québec: Les Presses de l'Université Laval, 1983. *Les Archives de Folklore*: 24.

Santino, Jack. *All Around the Year: Holidays and Celebrations in American Life*. Urbana, Ill.: University of Illinois Press, 1994.

Sauermann, Dietmar, ed. *Ostern in Westfalen: Materialien zur Geschichte eines volkstümlichen Kirchenfestes*. Münster: F. Coppenrath Verlag, 1986.

Scharfe, Martin, ed. *Brauchforschung*. Darmstadt: Wissenschaftliche Buchgesellschaft, 1991.

Schmidt, Friedrich Heinz. *Osterbräuche*. Leipzig: Bibliographisches Institut, 1936.

Schmieder, Friedrich. "Psychologische und Psychohygienische Fragen bei der Fasnachtsforschung." In: *Fasnacht*, 99–106. Tübingen: Tübinger Vereinigung für Volkskunde, 1964.

Schultz, Uwe, ed. *Das Fest: Eine Kulturgeschichte von der Antike bis zur Gegenwart*. Munich: Verlag C. H. Beck, 1988. See especially Leander Petzold, "Narrenfeste, Fastnacht, Fasching, Karneval in der Bürgerkultur der frühen Neuzeit," pages 140–152.

Schwedt, Herbert, and Elke Schwedt. *Bräuche zwischen Saar und Sieg: Zum Wandel der Festkulten in Rheinland-Pfalz und im Saarland*. Mainz: Gesellschaft für Volkskunde in Rheinland-Pfalz, 1989.

Seebach, Helmut. *Alte Feste in der Pfalz*. Vol. 2, *Fastnacht: Ein Beitrag zur Fastnachtsforschung und zur oberdeutschschweizerischen Einwanderung in die Pfalz*. Mainz-Gonsenheim: Bachstelz-Verlag Helmut Seebach, 1997.

Shoemaker, Alfred L. *Eastertide in Pennsylvania: A Folk-Cultural Study*. 1st ed. Kutztown, Pa.: Pennsylvania Folklife Society, 1960.

Smith, Robert Jerome. "Festivals and Celebrations." In: *Folklore and Folklife: An Introduction*, edited by Richard M. Dorson, 159–172. Chicago: University of Chicago Press, 1972.

Spamer, Adolf. *Deutsche Fastnachtsbräuche*. Jena: E. Diederichs, 1936.

———, ed. *Die Deutsche Volkskunde*. 2 vols. Leipzig: Bibliographisches Institut, 1934.

Strobl, Andreas. *Ovum Paschale novum, oder, Neugefärbte Oster-Ayr, das ist, Viertzig geistliche Discurs auff den H. Ostertag und Ostermontag*. Saltzburg: Melchior Haan, 1694.

Sund, Horst, ed. *Fastnacht in Geschichte, Kunst und Literatur*. Konstanz: Universitätsverlag, 1984.

ter Laan, K. *Folkloristisch Woordenboek van Nederland en Vlaams België*. The Hague: Batavia, 1949.

Tokofsky, Peter Ian. "The Rules of Fools: Carnival in Southwest Germany." Ph.D. diss. in Folklore and Folklife, University of Pennsylvania, 1992.

Turner, Victor, ed. *Celebration: Studies in Festivity and Ritual*. Washington, D.C.: Smithsonian Institution Press, 1982.

Van Gennep, Arnold. *Manuel de folklore français contemporain*. Paris: A. Picard, 1943–1951.

Warren, Nathan B. *The Holidays: Christmas, Easter, and Whitsuntide; Their Social Functions, Customs, and Carols*. New York: Hurd and Houghton, 1868.

Watts, Alan W. *Easter: Its Story and Meaning*. London: Abelard-Schuman, 1959.

———. *Myth and Ritual in Christianity*. London: Thames and Hudson, 1954.

Weaver, William Woys. *Pennsylvania Dutch Country Cooking*. New York: Abbeville, 1993. Contains two fastnacht recipes from the Mahantongo Valley in Schuylkill County.

Weber-Kellermann, Ingeborg. *Saure Wochen Frohe Feste: Fest und Alltag in der Sprache der Bräuche*. Munich: Verlag C. J. Bucher, 1985.

———. *Volksfeste in Deutschland*. Hamburg: HB-Bildatlas Spezial, 1981.

Weber-Kellermann, Ingeborg, and Andreas C. Bimmer. *Einführung in die Volkskunde/Europäische Ethnologie: Eine Wissenschaftsgeschichte*. 2d ed. Stuttgart: J. B. Metzlersche Verlagsbuchhandlung, 1985.

Weidkuhn, Peter. "Ideologiekritisches zum Streit zwischen Fasnacht und Protestantismus in Basel." *Schweizerisches Archiv für Volkskunde* 65 (1969): 36–74.

Weinhold, Gertrud. *Das schöne Osterei in Europa*. Kassel: J. P. Hinnenthal, 1965.

Wentz, Richard E., ed. *Pennsylvania Dutch Folk Spirituality*. New York: Paulist Press, 1993.

Wildhaber, Robert, ed. "Osterbrauchtum in Europa." *Schweizerisches Archiv für Volkskunde* 53, nos. 2, 3 (1957): 61–204.

———. "Zum Symbolgehalt und zur Ikonographie des Eies." *Deutsches Jahrbuch für Volkskunde* 6 (1960): 77–84.

Wuchter, A. C. "Fahsnacht." In: *Horne's Pennsylvania German Manual*, 3d ed., [edited] by A. R. Horne, 165–168. Allentown, Pa.: T. K. Horne, 1905.

Yoder, Don. *Discovering American Folklife: Studies in Ethnic, Religious, and Regional Culture*. Ann Arbor, Mich.: UMI Research Press, 1990.

———, tr. and ed. *The Picture-Bible of Ludwig Denig: A Pennsylvania German Emblem Book*. 2 vols. New York: Hudson Hills Press in association with the Museum of American Folk Art and the Pennsylvania German Society, 1990. Includes a series of fraktur drawings of the Passion, Crucifixion, Resurrection, and Ascension.

———, ed. "Symposium on Folk Religion." *Western Folklore* 33, no. 1 (January 1974): 1–87.

Yoder, Don, and Thomas E. Graves. *Hex Signs: Pennsylvania Dutch Barn Symbols and Their Meaning*. 2d ed., rev. and exp. Mechanicsburg, Pa.: Stackpole Books, 2000. For a detailed account on continuity theories, see the chapter entitled "The Scholars' War" on pages 11–18.

Index